# A STRATEGY

## FOR

## THE FUTURE

For my dear
friend Jack with
heartiest best wishes
for a happy
1977.

M. R.

# Books by Ervin Laszlo

Essential Society

Individualism Collectivism and Political Power

Beyond Scepticism and Realism

Philosophy in the Soviet Union
(EDITED)

The Communist Ideology in Hungary

System Structure and Experience

Human Values and Natural Science
(EDITED, WITH J. B. WILBUR)

La Metaphysique de Whitehead

Human Dignity: This Century and the Next
(EDITED, WITH R. GOTESKY)

Human Values and the Mind of Man
(EDITED, WITH J. B. WILBUR)

Evolution and Revolution
(EDITED, WITH R. GOTESKY)

Introduction to Systems Philosophy

The Relevance of General Systems Theory
(EDITED)

The World System: Models, Norms, Applications
(EDITED)

The Systems View of the World

Emergent Man: His Chances, Problems and Potentials
(EDITED, WITH J. STULMAN)

# A STRATEGY FOR THE FUTURE

.

*The Systems Approach to World Order*

ERVIN LASZLO

*George Braziller*     *New York*

Written Under the Auspices of
the Center of International Studies
Princeton University

For information, address the publisher:
George Braziller, Inc.
One Park Avenue, New York, N.Y. 10016

Standard Book Number: 0–8076–0743–6, cloth
0–8076–0744–4, paper

Library of Congress Catalog Card Number: 73–92679
First Printing
Printed in the United States of America

# INTRODUCTION

We cannot be optimistic about the future of the human species unless we envisage a rather drastic restructuring of social, economic, and political life on the planet. But as matters now stand the structure of global society seems rigidly confined by the logic of state sovereignty and its supportive ideology of nationalism. If anything, the overthrow of colonialism has strengthened the hold of the state system on the reins of power and authority in the last decade or so by giving rise to a large number of governments jealous of the traditional prerogatives of states. We confront, then, a dangerous kind of tension between what seems necessary and desirable and what seems possible.

One encouraging development is the increasing number of serious efforts to bridge this gap in such a way as to find the means to build the sort of world society that has the capacity to deal with the problems confronting humankind. Among these intellectual efforts none is more significant than the work of Ervin Laszlo, who has brought to bear the well-developed framework of general systems analysis on the specific task of constructing a just and viable system of world order. In A *Strategy for the Future*, Laszlo portrays with intellectual power and originality the contours of a desirable world system and provides a carefully interrelated conception of how we get from here to there.

Northrop Frye has noted that utopian thought is "less concerned with achieving ends than with visualizing possibilities." But Laszlo confutes traditional utopianism; he is deadly serious about achieving ends and regards the initiation of a process of global reform as the most important contribution that a scholar can presently make to the practical problems of human existence. Such seriousness is totally new in the intellectual history of utopian or reformist thought, as is the intellectual rigor with which Laszlo assesses the problems. World-order studies are, I think, with Laszlo's help being liberated from their literary and sentimental origins and achieving the status of a new academic discipline of normative content that deals with evidence, explanation, and prediction.

Too often world-order reformers have been inclined to write a constitution for the world and counsel for its adoption. Such legalism and moralism turns off more people than it turns on. It seems hopelessly preachy and naïve, lacking either a sense of evil or a strategy of change. Laszlo is admirably sensitive to these pitfalls. His proposals wisely refrain from including a definite blueprint of the future. Indeed, one creative dimension of his approach is to tell us how we can begin to participate in a process of designing the future.

As with other system theorists, Laszlo stresses information flow, the process of inquiry, and relies on steerage or guidance metaphors to provide the basis for planetary restructuring. In this respect, the approach is much more radical than is customary in the literature of political science or global reform. For Laszlo's approach concentrates upon encouraging the participation of individuals and groups at all levels of social organization in the formation of policy that is beneficial for the planet as a whole. His world-order solution is really quite "platonic," envisioning a knowledge-based guidance system rather than a supergovernment.

If Laszlo's approach takes hold, bureaucracies, armies, even police become less omnipresent, not more so, as we move toward the realization of an adequate network to support the global coordination we require to deal with problems of peace, poverty, oppression, pollution, and resource shortage.

But is this a credible scenario of future developments? How do potential recruits in a world-order movement circumvent the many obstacles that now block the road to global reform? How does such a movement mobilize enough energy to reorganize the world system without first gaining control over the apparatus of the state in most of the important countries of the world? Laszlo is responsive to these central issues. He places great stress in the immediate period upon opportunities for consciousness-raising with respect both to the agenda of challenges and to possible directions of response. Laszlo believes, in effect, that global integration is an idea whose time has come, indeed that the only major uncertainty concerns its auspices and effects. Thus, Laszlo believes that the growing seriousness of the main world-order problems—malnutrition and famine, recurrent warfare, environmental decay, crowding, resource shortages—will increasingly imprint itself upon the social consciousness of individuals and groups until even governments are forced to seek solutions. The special quality of Laszlo's approach, what sets it apart on matters of substance, is his coherent view of a normatively oriented information process, based on the image of "the town meeting," acting at all levels of human interaction to relate behavior to norms selected to serve planetary well-being and human dignity.

In effect, we are given a plausible and comprehensive nonviolent populist strategy for drastic global reform. The end product would be a largely self-regulating global arrangement, depicted by Laszlo in institutional terms and oriented around the ethics of humanism. The dynamics of the process do not depend initially on convincing governments to act in a reasonable or humane way. Such an unwarranted expectation has often infected the bloodstream of global-reform thinking with a flabbiness of vision of the sort one associates with the more doctrinaire versions of world federalism.

I don't think we come away from Laszlo's book with a sense

of either complacency or optimism. Indeed, if I understand him, he is trying to enlist, as a matter of urgent priority, the most creative and dedicated minds around the world in the collaborative work of building a new consciousness about the future of human society. What Laszlo provides, then, is a framework based on systems theory that can accommodate information drawn from any discipline or perspective and an insistence that the future of the human race is too important to be left in the hands of statesmen, generals, cartelists, and the like—who, in any event, are disastrously confined by the predispositions and interest structure of the state system.

Perhaps, Laszlo does not yet fully enough address issues of economic and political exploitation in a manner that will satisfy or convince all his readers. I believe, for instance, that the rise of neo-Darwinian geopolitics and attitudes is the most likely short-term response to the inadequacy of the state system. Already there are murmurings in the West that Arab oil boycotts of 1973 are hostile acts, even acts of war, and that maybe it will be necessary and justifiable to occupy the oil fields before long and administer them as "an international trust"! As scarcities grow more acute the powerful and rich can be expected to wage a ruthless struggle to sustain their position. Freedom of information, on which so much of Laszlo's approach depends, may be (some would argue, already is) an early casualty in this struggle. Few governing elites today allow their citizens the liberty needed to explore new social, economic, or political options. Consciousness-raising may have to be an underground activity in most of the world for quite a long time.

But in the end I believe Laszlo has put us on the right track in an innovative and exciting way. His leadership in the systems area is itself one element in a new movement for global reform taking place among intellectuals throughout the world. In my view, anyone concerned with the future of humankind and eager to take part in its creation has a special obligation to read what Laszlo has written. His book deserves to be one of the main texts for the reeducation of the mind that must occur if we are ever to become both good citizens and good people.

RICHARD A. FALK
*Princeton University*

# CONTENTS

INTRODUCTION BY RICHARD A. FALK      v

PREFACE      xiii

## PART ONE
### The Systems Approach to World Order

1. ANATOMY OF THE NEXT CONCEPTUAL SYNTHESIS      3
   The Need for Conceptual Synthesis      3
   Prospects for a Scientific Synthesis      11
   The Promise of General Systems Theory      15

2. THE SYSTEMS VIEW OF FUTURE WORLD ORDER      21
   Four Criteria for Theories of World Order      21
   Framework for a General Systems Theory of World Order      28
   Norms for a Future World Order      41

## PART TWO
### A Strategy for the Future

3. THE INDIVIDUAL AND WORLD ORDER:
   THE STRATEGY OF POPULAR INVOLVEMENT      65
   The "Can" Problem      66
   The "Ought" Problem      79

4. PHASE ONE: THE RAISING OF
   WORLD–SYSTEM CONSCIOUSNESS      84
   Objectives of the First Phase      85
   Implementation of the Objectives      88
   A Scenario for Transition      104

5. PHASE TWO: THE ECOFEEDBACK
   INFORMATION–DECISION FLOW      111
   The Ecofeedback Concept      112
   Ecofeedback and Biofeedback      116
   Simulation of the Normative World      119
   The Response Mechanisms      129
   A Scenario for Transition      132

6. PHASE THREE: THE WORLD HOMEOSTAT SYSTEM    143
   *Design for a World Homeostat*    144
   *A Scenario for Transition*    176

7. GLOBAL HOMEOSTASIS: AN EVALUATION OF
   THE MEANS AND THE ENDS    183
   *Toward Global Homeostasis*    183
   *The Strategies of Meeting the Need*    184
   *Evaluation of the Means*    185
   *Evaluation of the Ends*    192
   *Beyond the World Homeostat System*    198

## *Appendix*

A REVIEW OF THE RELEVANT HYPOTHESES OF
GENERAL SYSTEMS THEORY    203
   *The Evolution of Complexity*    203
   *Systemic Invariance*    209

NOTES    227

INDEX    233

# PREFACE

Most human societies are presently moving into a new age of social, political, economic, and cultural existence. The coming age is characterized by increasing economic and political interdependence, the filling up of habitable space, the overcrowding of urban regions, the deterioration of the quality of the environment, the dwindling of nonrenewable energy and other resources, the evolution of electronic technologies, and the development of global-destruction capabilities. Many societies are already moving from an industrial-national, to a postindustrial-global mode of life. Comparable shifts have occurred previously in history, with the coming of the Neolithic as well as the First Industrial Revolution, and each transformation was unprecedented.

The last major transformation, the advent of the nation-state–dominated industrial age, caused much suffering and social maladjustment. It inspired conflicting views of man and society, as expressed in the democratic idea of laissez-faire and the socialist idea of a state-controlled economy. The Western world was divided against itself, and against the rest of the world. We still feel the aftermath of our experiments in trying to live with the industrial-national age. However, we are already on the threshold of a new age, which promises to be no less, indeed considerably more, difficult. We shall have to learn to live with a finite world which permits growth only to the limits of our technologies and wisdom.

Unless we develop new technologies, and the wisdom to manage our societies, our environment, and our lives, more people will suffer in the coming decades than ever before. The more potent our technologies, the more exploited our resources, the larger our numbers, and the more destructive our weapons, the greater the number of people who will suffer from mismanagement and conflict. We live on a scale incomparably larger than any previous civilization, but our wisdom is not proportionately enlarged. It is not difficult to see that what we need today, perhaps more than anything else, is applicable knowledge: the knowledge to live in the post-industrial-global civilization. This we cannot obtain by history alone, or statistics alone, or theories alone. We can obtain it, if at all, only by careful yet uninhibited inquiry into the general patterns of human life and society, their conditions of existence, and their alternatives for the future. The way to come to terms with our present predicament is to construct reasonable, empirically based but theoretically reconstructed *strategies for the future.*

One such strategy is presented in the pages of this book. It explores the avenue offered by the application of what is now widely known as General Systems Theory, or Systems Philosophy, to the study of world order. What this theory is will become evident as the reader peruses the first few chapters. What world order may be should be said at the outset. It is not merely a new "in" term for international relations theory or world politics. It is, rather, a new conceptualization in a field that embraces global ecology, geopolitics, human geography, international relations theory, anthropology, political science, and social ethics and philosophy. It is an attempt to grasp the contemporary situation on this planet in all its diversity without erecting, or conserving, artificial frontiers either between geographic or disciplinary territories. If we live on one planet which our electronically transmitted messages gird seven times a second, any and perhaps all regions of which our nuclear technologies can irreversibly destroy in a matter of minutes, and which we can behold as a whole in photographs transmitted from space, we must begin to think of it as one world with an order which, however diverse, informs all its parts.

Such thinking is world-order thinking. If we engage in it seriously, we can learn to distinguish various types of order, ranged in terms of human desirability and extending from an order that means disaster for the greater part of our populations, through orders that permit various degrees of survival and well-being, to some ideal order where the good life is available to all. Given a real possibility that world order may deteriorate dramatically within our lifetime, and the further possibility that we may have means at our disposal to reverse such a trend, few tasks could be more important than exploring various approaches to the study of world order and systematically exploring the conceptions derivable from them.

This book is an attempt at exploring the potentials of the systems approach to the study of world order; in particular, at discovering the norms for a desirable world order suggested by a consistent application of systems principles to global conditions. It is a first approximation and is meant to stimulate further efforts in this area rather than provide a finished product. Writing and researching it has been an exciting adventure, highlighted by challenging discussions with students and faculty at my 1973 series of Colloquia on "Systems Philosophy and World Order" at the Center of International Studies, Princeton University. I would like to thank all those who took part in these discussions, for they contributed more to the writing of this book than they perhaps suspect. I am especially grateful for the stimulating contributions of Richard Falk, Harold Sprout, Alastair Taylor, Gerald Garvey, and Cyril Black. It is a pleasure to acknowledge here the efficient help of Mary Merrick and Dorothy Dey of the Princeton staff in preparing the first draft of the manuscript, and of Jane

McDowall for meticulously proofreading it. And I should like to thank my wife, who has not only put up with, but has constantly encouraged, an absent-minded and occasionally despairing spouse during the hectic but exciting spring of 1973, when the bulk of the work on this venture was completed.

E. L.

# PART ONE

.

*The Systems Approach to*
*World Order*

# 1

---

# ANATOMY OF THE NEXT
# CONCEPTUAL SYNTHESIS

## The Need for Conceptual Synthesis

Every age has produced a synthesis of its most trusted items of knowledge. The synthesis has been more or less explicit, far-ranging and logical; and it has had various success in satisfying the cognitive needs and practical problems of its age. But there has never been an age of human civilization without some degree of integration in its fields of knowledge and the use of the integrated system in the guidance of its practical affairs.

Ours is perhaps the most diversified, least integrated, and most diffusely applied body of knowledge mankind has yet produced. It is also the most exact one in specific, fragmented areas, and the most operational. That it has produced the greatest disorder in the terrestrial household of man is little wonder. It is likewise obvious that unless we integrate and focus our knowledge the disorder will grow into disaster.

Without a synthesis of the items of knowledge held valid in a society, no individual or collective long-term purposes can be identified and rationally pursued. The more precise the knowledge system, the sharper the dynamics of the human processes oriented toward identified goals and conscious purposes. In the past, the synthesis of knowledge was based on items accepted on faith and handed down in the culture's traditions. Even such syntheses faced concrete tasks in the orientation of action, since bodies of knowledge which gave consistently false directions were soon phased out in the process of natural selection acting on the biological bases of culture systems: the misdirected population was assimilated in more viable cultures, or faced extinction.

This is not to say that every viable synthesis produced universal satisfaction; merely that it offered sufficiently tested orientations to enable the population subscribing to it to survive. A group of conscious beings will not rely on instincts alone any more than on blind habit and unreflected tradition. Every major decision is justified in terms of a knowledge scheme, but every knowledge scheme is tentative and open to reexamination. Ineffective knowledge schemes are either replaced, or the population suffers for their continued beliefs. Viable civilizations constantly modify their syntheses to keep them functional. Thus a long sequence of conceptual syntheses unfolds in history, each scheme holding sway for a time, to be succeeded by more updated and efficient modes of thought and views of the world.

In the ancient Western world, great writings, committed to paper and copied by learned scholars, served as pivotal points of the synthesis of knowledge. There was the Jewish Bible, the epics of Homer and the *Theogony* of Hesiod, the works of Aristotle, and the *encyclopaedias* of Varro and Pliny. In the Middle Ages these syntheses of classical knowledge were elaborated by Christendom and Islam. The former produced Augustine's *City of God*, Justinian's *Corpus Juris Civilis*, the *Etymologies* of Isidore, and the *Summae* of Thomas Aquinas. Islam produced the Koran and such works as Al–Farabi's *Book of Traditions*, Avicenna's *Book of Recovery*, and Ibn Khaldun's *Universal History*.

Oriental civilizations produced their own syntheses of

knowledge, and their own great texts stating particular formulations. In ancient India, the major syntheses were stated in the *Vedas*, the *Upanishads*, the *Puranas*, the *Bhagavad Gita*, and the works of six major schools of Hindu philosophy. In China the great expressions of synthesized knowledge were the Confucian canon, the systematic historical records of Ssu-ma Ch'ien and his successors, and encyclopedias such as the *T'ai-ping yü-lan* of Wu Shu and Li Fang.

But in the eighteenth century, the harmonious synthesis of Christianity, in the works of the great scholastics, broke apart. The originators of modern science—Galileo, Descartes, Boyle, Hooke, Pascal, Kepler, and Newton—viewed the scientific endeavor as a special service of man on behalf of the Christian God and saw no contradiction between their findings and the precepts of religious tradition. But the seemingly harmonious edifice that housed both science and the Christian synthesis began to show signs of strain with the views held by Bruno and Galileo. The kind of distinction between quantities and qualities claimed by Galileo logically led to the empiricism of Hume and Locke. Books that did not deal with quantifiable facts were to be committed to the flames, as Hume advocated in his famous statement. This meant the greater part of the accumulated texts stating the religious synthesis of the West.

While Hume, in company with other philosophers such as Kant and Berkeley, did try to reconcile the ethical principles of human nature (essentially those of Western civilization) with the factual foundations of the new natural sciences, the radical wing of the French Enlightenment had no patience for such halfway measures. De la Mettrie proclaimed man to be a machine; Condorcet suggested a judiciary system based on the calculus of probability, and Holbach proposed a mechanistic and materialistic "system of nature." Against these scientific views the great intellects of the eighteenth and nineteenth centuries rose in arms. Goethe, Nietzsche, Hegel,

Schiller and Schopenhauer attempted syntheses based on the primacy of human, and humanistic, components. But the great rift was too deep to be healed by insightful philosophies from either end. The Western conceptual synthesis became split into a "natural philosophy" specified as a natural science (which the social sciences tried increasingly to emulate) and a "moral philosophy" which embraced the traditional branches of philosophy including ethics and metaphysics.

When, in the nineteenth century, the first industrial revolution broke over the West and large-scale suffering and disorientation prompted concerned thinkers to provide a dependable foundation for social change, Hegel's great idealistic synthesis was transposed by Marx along materialistic lines to accord with the then current scientific revolutions: Darwinian theory of evolution, the new chemistry of Priestley and Lavoisier, and Schwann's theory of the cellular basis of life. In the late nineteenth and early twentieth centuries social unrest led to the institutionalization of the Marxian synthesis with new elements infused mainly by Lenin. Although the Russian people came under the spell of the conceptual synthesis of Marxism-Leninism—a new religion where matter instead of spirit was God and motion rather than ideas were eternal—most Western societies learned to live with a world view fundamentally split into scientific and religious-moral components. Oriental civilizations came increasingly in contact with the Western world through faster and broader channels of communication, trade, and transportation, and partly surrendered, partly shifted their own integrated conceptual systems to accommodate the new influences.

Presently all boundaries between cultures are rapidly disintegrating. It will no longer be possible to simultaneously uphold several incompatible conceptual syntheses valid for different people at different places. Our bodies of knowledge are as interdependent as our patterns of life. There is only one science for East and West, and though there are many religions and belief systems, they are becoming insignificant in terms of their influence on the operative knowledge of the age.

We are headed toward a global civilization and, as all previous, smaller-scale civilizations have, it too will produce a conceptual synthesis. This synthesis can also be more or less explicit, far-ranging, and logical, and it can have more or less success in satisfying concrete needs for guidance in the processes of human affairs. We cannot see into the future and predict what the nature and success of the synthesis of the coming world order will be like. But we can say that *if* the coming world order will be a viable one, its conceptual synthesis will be explicit, far-ranging, scientifically based, and pregnant with normative guidelines for practical behavior.

Conceptual syntheses perform at least five basic functions in the guidance of human affairs. They are the mystical, the cosmological, the sociological, the pedagogical or psychological, and the editorial functions.[1] The mystical function inspires in man a sense of mystery and profound meaning related to the existence of the universe and of himself in it. The cosmological function forms images of the universe in accord with local knowledge and experience, enabling men to describe and identify the structure of the universe and the forces of nature. The sociological function validates, supports, and enforces the local social order, representing it as in accord with the nature of the universe, or as the natural or right form of social organization. The pedagogical or psychological function guides individuals through the stages of life, teaching ways of understanding themselves and others and presenting desirable responses to life's challenges and trials. Finally, the editorial function of conceptual syntheses is to define some aspects of reality as important and credible and hence to be attended to, and other aspects as unworthy of serious attention.

In today's world, most of the traditional functions of cognitive syntheses have atrophied, and lie ignored and neglected. Mythology is currently relegated to the status of mere superstition; man is no longer inspired by a sense of mystery and profound meaning in life and the universe. Religions suffer from a credibility gap and concentrate increasingly on problems of community relations and social justice. Contemporary science has assumed the role of forming our images of the universe and of human nature, but its disclosures come in a highly disjoined, atomistic manner, and are wrapped in the esoteric jargon of mathematics and specialty languages.

Thus the meaning of scientific knowledge fails to penetrate the fabric of society. Bureaucrats and civil servants, who make no claim to understand or even to seek a larger picture of reality, carry out the sociological function of administering and enforcing local social orders. The pedagogical or educational function of guiding individuals through the stages of life has been relegated to secular institutions of mental health and psychotherapy, traditions having faltered, and then completely failed, in advanced industrial societies. The editorial function is now administered by technocrats, public relations experts, and the funding agencies which steer the processes of large-scale research and development. All these functions, insofar as they are performed, originate from separate groups with fragmented and often mutually incompatible world views. Aside from a few countries which are actively engaged in fighting for their existence or carrying out revolutions to catch up with their peers (e.g., Israel, North Vietnam, China), contemporary societies suffer from a lack of meaning and guidance, because of the atrophy and fragmentation of their conceptual syntheses. Alcoholism, drug addiction, suicide and divorce rates, crime and corruption, are sharply on the rise; a sense of purpose, a vital image of the future, and meaningful individual and societal goals are lacking. Persons seek their own interests through their social roles; wealth and power are the mainsprings of activity. The result is inefficiency in large organizations, and corruption among the political leadership.

Yet a sense of purpose beyond one's own narrow interests is desperately needed. There has hardly been another period in history when the need for transformation was so great, and the room for error so small, as today. Technological society creates progressively more problems and becomes increasingly more vulnerable in the process of coping with them. Our conceptual synthesis can no longer fail to perform on all counts or dictate partially counterfunctional patterns of behavior; insufficient and incorrect guidance results in breakdowns of catastrophic proportions, affecting the lives of millions. This is why the conceptual synthesis of the coming age will have to operate on all levels, and why its premises and its main inspiration will have to be based on the sciences.

By calling for a "scientific" synthesis we need not mean a universal worship of science and the view that all our knowledge is either derived from the sciences or is plainly nonsensical. That the inspiration of our conceptual synthesis must be based on science does not mean that it must be limited to the scope of contemporary validated scientific theories. It must extend, on the contrary, to all the functions which conceptual syntheses have traditionally performed. But inasmuch as it suggests guidelines for concrete action, it must respect the reduced error-tolerance of the contemporary situation; hence it must base itself on the empirically tested knowledge accumulated in the sciences. Science is a body of knowledge which is hallmarked by the fact that it is constantly tested against experience (as well as, to some extent, against rival theories) under controlled conditions. This fact recommends science as the mainspring of our conceptual synthesis in view of our reduced degrees of freedom in effecting the needed societal-cultural transformations. But it does not mean that we can afford to restrict our synthesis to science, for pure science makes a poor religion and an inadequate basis for morality, for existential meaning, and for individual and collective purpose. Our conceptual synthesis will have to be scientific at its core, but move beyond the concurrent reach of the sciences in satisfying our demands for coherence in the more esoteric regions of human experience. Binding the scientific and the spiritual domains, the new knowledge must remain coherent and self-consistent, replacing the incoherence and the tacit, as well as overt, contradictions traversing our existing scientific, religious, and moral systems of ideas.

The new conceptual synthesis cannot content itself with remaining a plaything of the mind, cherished and cultivated in isolated ivory towers of learning and culture. Ivory tower philosophy and "pure" science may continue to be pursued by a small number of researchers for the intrinsic values of gaining knowledge for the sake of knowledge, but the bulk of the conceptual synthesis will have to be moved by concerned investigators into the worldly arena of practical application. There, its task will be to suggest the norms by which the global civilization of man can be purposefully guided, and also the detailed processes whereby such guidance can be effected. Fragmented knowledge, even if deriving directly from the sciences, is incapable of fulfilling this task. It treats the many systematically interdependent factors of global existence as the separate domains of disciplinary territories, each jealously guarded by specialists well endowed with the instincts of cognitive territoriality. The human future can only be assured by a synthesis based on science but integrating the relevant pieces of scientific knowledge with one another, and thus integrating scientific knowledge with those insights that have been won without benefit of scientific method but which nevertheless have proven to be meaningful in themselves, and valuable in guiding the imagination and focusing the thrust of human motivation.

## Prospects for a Scientific Synthesis

Although a fully scientific conceptual synthesis is unlikely to occur in the foreseeable future (and could occur in the distant future only if many phenomena now recalcitrant to quantitative measurement and prediction become accessible to scientific treatment), the chances of producing a scientific synthesis sufficient to provide the basis for a general conceptual synthesis are good. This moderately optimistic assessment is based on two observations: first, on an intrinsic trend within science itself to maximize the scope of theories consistently with their precision; second, on extrinsic pressures on science for transcending traditional disciplinary boundaries in producing coherent and applicable bodies of knowledge.

(I) Modern science has made great progress by adopting the basically analytic method of identifying and if possible isolating the phenomena to be investigated. If effective isolation is not feasible (for example, in the life and the social sciences), it is replaced by the theoretical device of averaging the values of inputs and outputs to the investigated object, and varying the quantities with the needs of the experiment. Thus influences from what has often been disparagingly called "the rest of the world" can be disregarded. It appears, however, that "the rest of the world" is an important factor in many areas of investigation. The consequences of disregarding it are not immediately evident, for a good detailed knowledge of the immediate phenomena in a short time-range can nevertheless be won. But the spin-offs, or side effects, of the phenomena will be incalculable, and such effects are not the secondary phenomena they were taken to be in the past. They are the results of the complex strands of interdependence which traverse all realms of empirical investigation but which science's analytic method selectively filters out. Hence we get much detailed knowledge of local phenomena, and a great deal of ignorance of the interconnections between such phenomena.

The analytic method produced the explosion of contemporary scientific *information* and the dearth of applicable scientific *knowledge*. It has also engendered wasteful parallelisms in research due to failures in the transfer of models and data between disciplines. Yet to many scientists and philosophers of science, the advantages of specialization outweigh its disadvantages, and they are not discouraged by the prospect of further specialization and segmentation in the evolution of science.

However, there are factors operating within the scientific enterprise which correct for the deficiencies of overspecialization through the development of new, more integrated theoretical frameworks. Modern science has had long experience in dealing with explosions of data and proliferations of theory, and was quite successful in containing them in the past. Galileo, Kepler, and Newton provided broad conceptual schemes for integrating observations in physics and astronomy; Darwin provided the master scheme for biology. When the Newtonian synthesis encountered anomalies, Einstein proposed a new framework for reinterpreting data in a more consistent and integrated manner. Scientists have always sought, in Einstein's words, "the simplest possible system of thought which will bind together the observed facts."[2] From Kepler, who had hopes of understanding the Plan of Creation, to Heisenberg, who despite the complexities of quantum physics maintained that what the physicist seeks is to penetrate more and more reality as a great interconnected whole,[3] we can perceive a search for theories that respond to the scientist's appreciation of elegance and accuracy combined with integral scope and extensibility to neighboring fields and as yet uninvestigated phenomena. Theories are required to be "fertile" not only in explaining and predicting already known observations and processes, but in generating specifying theorems which can deal with new observations and presently recalcitrant or anomalous processes. This requirement blurs the distinction between discovery and invention, and moves contemporary science beyond the traditional confines of classical empiricism and its neopositivist restatement.

It is instructive to review the contributions of great theoretical scientists in reference to the degree of integration, abstraction, and generality which they introduced in their field.[4] Scientists value theory-refinement as well as theory-extension, although they do so to differing degrees. The routine experimentalist, mainly involved with puzzles that can be solved through a suitable application of existing theories and techniques, tends to disparage the "philosophizing" of colleagues bent on the revision and refinement of the theories themselves.[5] But scientists who perceive internal inconsistencies in their frameworks of explanation are greatly concerned with overcoming them through the creation of new, more general postulates, embracing existing theories as special cases, or reinterpreting them in the light of new axioms.

Although the emphasis changes from person to person, scientific community to scientific community, and from period to period depending on the problems encountered in the given field, it remains true that, on the whole, the progress of science involves the integration of loosely joined lower-level concepts and hypotheses in mathematically formulated general theories. As Conant says, two streams of human activity, separated until the sixteenth century, gradually came together. These were abstract reasoning, as represented by Euclidean geometry, and experimentation, represented by the work of the metallurgists who over the generations had improved the methods of winning metals from the ores. As a result, we can view science as "a dynamic undertaking directed to lowering the degree of empiricism in solving problems; or . . . a process of fabricating a web of interconnected concepts and conceptual schemes arising from experiments and observations and fruitful of further experiments and observations."[6]

(II) The historical trend in science is to counterbalance segmentation and specialization in patterns of research and experimentation. However, when great progress is made by means of specialized research, corrective measures could be suspended for decades or even centuries; hopes for a scientific synthesis would be dim if we had to rely on trends intrinsic to science alone. But a powerful ally of the theoretician's dream of elegant and integrated theories has emerged in recent years in the guise of an extrinsic demand on science to deliver theories capable of societal application. This demand unfolds as a consequence of the excessive fragmentation of scientific data with respect to operational utility. For example, our knowledge of the environment is segmented into academic compartments, but the environmental factors themselves form an interdependent continuum. As a result there has been a marked shift in public support for scientific projects.

The new pattern of allocations favors research that has social utility either by having direct applications, or by clarifying norms or techniques relevant to applications. At the same time, the meaning of applied science has been vastly enlarged. It is no longer restricted to the design of labor-saving devices, machines, and processes for the manufacture and distribution of goods. Applied science has come to include the "software" of social technologies as well, including the principles of administration and management, policy sciences, and the behavioral applications of individual and group psychology.

The new patterns of resource allocation reflect society's rising need for a scientific synthesis of its socially applicable bodies of knowledge. Such bodies of knowledge seldom result from research carried out within the compartments of traditional scientific disciplines. In almost every case, concrete societal problems call for interdisciplinary research, and the integration of hitherto separately investigated variables.

There are no problems that can be fully resolved without impacting at the same time on the resolution or aggravation of other problems—as Garrett Hardin said, we can never do "just one thing." We live on a finite planet and constantly increase our interdependence among ourselves, as well as our dependence upon the earth's biological and energy resources. Disciplinary compartmentalization is useful only if it is coupled with transdisciplinary integration. This demand is not likely to eliminate specialized research for the sake of gathering knowledge independently of its potential of application, for such research continues to be an ideal of science and, beyond that, of human civilization. But the scientific enterprise as a whole is likely to feel the effects of societal pressures for applicable knowledge, and these effects will include a relative de-emphasis on specialized research for the sake of pure knowledge, and a strong emphasis on all research that can jointly produce operational results.

## The Promise of General Systems Theory

A general theory of the many kinds of systems investigated in the natural and social sciences arose recently in response to the contemporary need to counterbalance fragmentation and duplication in scientific research. Von Bertalanffy, justly regarded as its founder, summed up the aims of general systems theory in reference to the following points:

(1) There is a general tendency toward integration in the various sciences, natural and social.
(2) Such integration seems to be centered in a general theory of systems.
(3) Such theory may be an important means for aiming at exact theory in the nonphysical fields of science.
(4) Developing unifying principles running 'vertically' through

the universe of the individual sciences, this theory brings us nearer to the goal of the unity of science.

(5) This can lead to a much needed integration in scientific education.[7]

In view of contemporary needs in the practical domains, we may add,

(6) Bringing us closer to the unity of science and the integration of scientific education, this theory could provide a basis for a conceptual synthesis capable of fulfilling the time-honored, but presently unfulfilled functions of conceptual guidance and individual and collective motivation.

The stated aims of the society created to promote general systems thinking, the Society for General Systems Research, include corresponding ideals:

(1) To investigate the isomorphy of concepts, laws, and models in various fields, and to help useful transfers from one field to another.

(2) To encourage the development of adequate theoretical models in fields which lack them.

(3) To minimize the duplication of theoretical effort in different fields.

(4) To promote the unity of science through improving communication among specialists.[8]

To these aims, also, we propose adding another,

(5) To promote and encourage the application of unified scientific knowledge in the area of concrete societal problems, for the benefit of individuals, societies, and mankind generally.

In fact, the society has been increasingly concerned with the application of general systems theory to various organizational and societal problems. This new emphasis is manifest in the society's annual meetings, in the nature of the articles appearing in the *General Systems Yearbook* and in the newly affiliated journal *Behavioral Science*.

General systems theory, like other innovative frameworks of thought, passed through phases of ridicule and neglect. It has benefited, however, from the parallel emergence and rise to eminence of cybernetics and information theory, and their widespread applications to originally quite unsuspected fields. Presently the rise of systems theory is aided by societal pressures on science calling for the development of theories capable of interdisciplinary application. General systems theory grew out of organismic biology, and has soon branched into most of the life and behavioral sciences. Its recent applications include the areas of social work, mental health, the political sciences, and the humanities.[9] Its extension to the new field of studies rallying around the concept of "world-order research" is a logical next step.

The specific contribution of general systems theory derives from its de-emphasis of traditional concepts of matter, substance, idea or spirit, and its explicit orientation toward grasping phenomena in terms of *organization.* "Organization" may be loosely defined as structure (in space) and function (in time). Structure and function are not rigorously separable, however. Structure is the record of past functions and the source of present ones. Function in turn is the behavior of structure and the pathway leading to the formation of new structures. The relativity of the concepts derives from the dominance of the concept of organization. Not what a thing is, what it is made of, or for what purpose it exists, defines it, but how it is organized. Its organization specifies the internal relations of the events which constitute it, and the external relations of the constituted entity to other entities in its environment.

The simplest conceptualization of an entity defined by its organizational invariance is *system.* A system in this definition is a collection of parts conserving some identifiable set of (internal) relations, with the summed relations (i.e., the system itself) conserving some identifiable set of (external) relations to other entities (systems).

The definition tightens considerably when we consider that if any set of events conserves identifiable sets of internal relations, it must be endowed with the characteristics of pattern-maintenance, i.e., it must be capable of at least temporarily withstanding the statistical outcome of disorganization predicted by the second law of thermodynamics. There must be organizing forces or relations present which permit the conservation of structure (and function). Internal relations in an entity not possessing such characteristics tend to degrade until a state of thermodynamical equilibrium is reached. An entity that does not degrade its structure to thermodynamical equilibrium, but maintains it through the utilization of energies available in its environment, is a product of the slow but vast processes of evolution in nature. It has emerged in the course of time, maintains itself in the face of perturbations, and is capable of reorganizing itself to cope with changing environments. Such an entity is a *natural system*. It may be contrasted with entities which obey the statistical predictions of the entropy law unless they are purposively maintained by an outside agency. These are not products of nature but human artefacts: *artificial systems*.

The noteworthy fact is that almost all the things we can identify as "the furniture of the earth" are natural systems, or parts of natural systems, or aggregates formed by natural systems. Stable atoms are natural systems, and so are molecules, cells, multicellular organisms, and ecologies. We shall argue that complex human sociocultural systems, and indeed the global system itself, form natural (rather than artificial) systems. This is important, for certain general propositions are true of natural systems, regardless of their size, origin, and complexity, which may not be true of artificial systems. These propositions are true in virtue of the fact that in a universe governed by uniform laws certain sets of relationships are required to conserve and enhance order over time. Much can be understood of the system's basic "nature" by assessing its behavior in reference to the imperatives of natural system dynamics.

The promise of general systems theory consists in (1) discerning natural systems in diverse areas of investigation, i.e., identifying those real entities which can be analyzed in terms of general system laws, (2) providing an inventory of natural systems from atoms to ecologies and possibly to social systems and the world system, (3) formulating the general principles accounting for the evolution of systems on multiple hierarchic levels, crossing the boundaries of the inorganic-organic, the organic-multiorganic, and their many subdivisions, and (4) referring chosen problems of philosophic-scientific-humanistic interest to the systems analysis of the relevant phenomena, carried out in the context of the integrated scheme of hierarchically organized natural systems.

Thus if *world order* is (4) the chosen problem of philosophic-scientific-humanistic interest, the task of general systems theory is to (1) inquire whether the world system can be identified as a natural system, (2) place the analysis of the world system in the context of the repertory of natural systems, taking into account (3) general principles of organic-multiorganic evolution. This method can relate the description of observed phenomena to the dynamics of viable natural systems by determining whether the structures and functions observed of the phenomena correspond to the preconditions of persistence and development of such systems. In the area of multihuman systems, the investigation can yield norms of conduct, values, and life-styles, as well as norms of social, economic, cultural, and political organization. This passage from "is" to "ought" is based on the premise of "if—then": *if* the chosen system is to persist and actualize its potentials, *then* certain conditions of structure and function must be met. The question can then be raised whether they are in fact met. And strategies for rectifying the situation may be evolved.*

If general systems theory can unfold its full promise, it could constitute the scientific core of the broad and yet rigorous conceptual synthesis we shall need in the coming decades. It can already furnish an interpretation of the problems of the present world order and disclose the norms for a more desirable one. This real potential of the general systems approach will be explored in the remainder of this book.

---

* The question can also be raised whether persons *ought* to concern themselves with rectifying the situation. This aspect of the normative problem is addressed in Chapter 3.

# 2

# THE SYSTEMS VIEW OF
# FUTURE WORLD ORDER

## Four Criteria for Theories of World Order

The contemporary social sciences find themselves in a pre-paradigm phase where different, and often incompatible theoretical conceptions compete and claim paradigmatic status. As Conant observed, many social scientists "would not dissent too strongly from the proposition that their whole area of investigation is in a state comparable to that of the biological sciences (including medicine) a hundred or a hundred and fifty years ago."[1] If this is the case, the social sciences should witness great strides forward in the next decades. Whether they in fact will make such strides is impossible to foretell with certainty. Yet it is quite likely that the social sciences will hit upon a working format for a general theory which will then be extended to explain, and within limits predict, social phenomena.

The motivation toward the creation of such theory is both internal and external to science, as previously discussed. But will the conceptual synthesis of the social sciences come in time? Will it be there to help us face the practical problems of choosing our steps among alternative possibilities, each with possibly irreversible long-term consequences? As long as the answer is in doubt, we must explore all reasonable avenues promising to lead to concretely applicable general theory in the social science fields.

The need for general theory is especially pronounced in the international relations field. Here orientations and objectives follow one another in rapid succession, without any of them establishing a lastingly dominant position. The theories themselves reflect the demands placed on the field by international developments. During the tenure of the League of Nations and the early phases of the United Nations, there have been the world federalists, world government theorists, and unifiers of the world. They were counterbalanced by the more skeptical if realistic analysts, like E. H. Carr on the left and Hans Morgenthau on the right, who updated and refined the balance-of-power doctrines during and after World War II. These were followed by the strategic thinkers who, facing the problems of nuclear balance in a polarized world, tried to find a rationale for deterrence and the politics of war while excluding recourse to full-scale warfare. After them came the grand strategists, like Herman Kahn and Brzezinski, and the world-system theorists, like Morton Kaplan. They conceived of the field of international relations as a vast system with stability properties determined by the confluence of several major geopolitical factors. The full swing of the pendulum from exclusive reliance on military power factors to concentration on the natural environment and its problems of space, quality, and resources, came with the writings of Harold and Margaret Sprout, and the computer projections of Forrester and Meadows, where the sphere of international relations is an interdependent natural system with finite and rapidly depleting resources.[2]

The single sustained trend in this checkered array of approaches and objectives is the movement of the strategic focus of inquiry from the level of the nation-state to that of the terrestrial world as a whole. As late as 1959 C. Wright Mills postulated the nation-state as "the most inclusive unit" which is both "history-making" and "man-making."[3] By 1971 Falk spoke of the same unit as embodying the outdated "logic of Westphalia" and lying at the root of the inadequacy of the present system of world order.[4] The emphasis now introduced by the Institute for World Order, and such international relations theorists as Knorr, Rosenau, and Singer, to mention but a few, consistently lifts the level of analysis to the world community as a whole.[5] Increasing interdependence, in military and economic power as well as in the resources needed to maintain such power, together with vastly increased intercommunication on multiple levels, makes such analysis better adapted to the problems than the formerly dominant focus on the internal and external affairs of nation-states.

There are neither epistemological nor ontological difficulties connected with the move from the nation-state to the world level of analysis. In regard to the epistemological problem, we may note that in any empirical situation the scientist is confronted with a mass of data that he seeks to order in theories. The method by which he chooses his theory determines the efficacy of his conclusions in explaining and predicting the events that engage his interest. Theories are underdetermined by data in the sense that no theory is uniquely specified by any set of observations or measurements. The choice among available theoretical frameworks must be made by comparing the explanatory and predictive power of each, together with such relatively amorphous factors as their simplicity, elegance, and ability to integrate data from different fields of inquiry. There is nothing intrinsically fallacious about constructing a model of the world community as a system with properties and dynamics of its own, provided one recognizes that such a model is not any more certain to be true than any of its rivals. There is no "immaculate perception" in any field of empirical investigation, and least of all in the international relations field.

Ontologically, there are cogent arguments in favor of endowing social entities above the nation-state level with the same existential reality granted to nation-states themselves. The boundaries of nation-states are not absolute walls but merely filters which operate in some regards and not in others. They impose gradients on the flow of persons insofar as restrictions on travel across national frontiers are in effect—and such is not always the case. They filter the flow of information if news censorship is in effect—likewise not always and effectively the case. They can impose limitations on the flow of material goods through import and export duties and quotas, and on political power through the privileges and obligations connected with the citizen's allegiance to his government.

But all these filters are partial at best, and in some cases they do not operate at all. Moreover the ecological processes of the earth do not respect national boundaries but move freely across them, influenced only by the geographic distribution of resources, and the technological extraction and dispersion processes which traverse the face of the globe. Electronic signals gird the circumference of the earth faster than seven times a second, and there are facilities for the transportation of persons and goods across almost all national frontiers. Moreover any point on earth can be programmed for nuclear devastation through long-range guided missiles, and all points are open to observation through stategically deployed satellites. In sum, the world no longer exists (if it ever did) as a conglomeration of atomic nation-states, bound only by external relations. The impartial observer—perhaps the legendary visitor from Mars—could note structural and functional units much larger than nations and perhaps as large as the globe's surface itself. He would see no reasons why models could not be proposed with full cogency of the world system as a whole.

If there are no reasons militating against the global level of conceptualization on epistemological and ontological grounds, we can point to definite advantages favoring such conceptualization on methodological grounds. These can be assessed in reference to the three requirements of international relations theory suggested by Singer, and the addition of one further requirement specifically for filling current needs. Singer's three criteria are accurate description, parsimonious explanation, and reliable prediction.[6] In regard to the requirement for accurate description, we may point out that the system level of analysis permits one to examine international relations as a whole, and generalize about such phenomena as the creation and dissolution of coalitions, the frequency and duration of specific power configurations, modifications in stability, responsiveness to changes in formal political institutions, and overall patterns of growth, decline, or equilibrium. The advantages of the world system level reside in the comprehensiveness of the analysis and the perception of patterns otherwise lost in the maze of data; its disadvantages derive entirely from a necessary dearth of detail.

Explanations flowing out of the world-level system model will be more parsimonious and manageable than the set of explanations required to account for analogous phenomena by reference to lower-level models. A model of the world system as a whole can average over the endogenous variables of its subsystems and treat them as functional components within the larger environment which is the world system itself. Thus on the one hand subsystems, such as nation-states, tend to recede into the background as black-boxes (a cost incurred by the high level of conceptualization), and on the other the functional input-output treatment of subsystems brings into focus the dynamics of interactions which would otherwise be obscured by the structural detail of the lower-level models of the diverse actors.

This benefit of the system level of analysis translates into a concrete payoff in providing a deductive basis for prediction. The variables required to account for the dynamics of international relations are endogenous in the systems level of analysis, and thus they are "under control" in the model. The very same variables are exogenous in the nation-state level of analysis, and thus function as uncontrolled environmental contingencies. Converting such exogenous variables into a dynamic sequence of determinate ordering would require the simultaneous integration of the outputs of many highly diverse national actors. This task is likely to tax the limits of lower-level models for some time to come. (It is analogous to providing a quantum mechanical explanation of the behavior of complex molecules. Theoretically it is possible, but in practice encounters difficulties of computation which may disqualify it as a way of giving coherent accounts of the structure, and especially of the time-dependent function, of such complex molecular substances as those involved in life phenomena.) Consequently, operating on the nation-state level of analysis, foreign policy decisions by national governments remain fraught with uncertainty, as Kissinger and other foreign policy specialists unfailingly remind us.

The system level of analysis in world affairs does provide definite advantages, as well as some necessary drawbacks, in relation to the three criteria of accurate description, parsimonious explanation, and reliable prediction. But we must add a fourth criterion of theory adequacy, specifically for the study of world order. It is stated as the requirement that world order theory provide not only descriptions and predictions, but also prescriptions, i.e., that it offer *norms* for the guidance of international behavior. In view of unstable and readily deteriorating global conditions, we must allow that world order models face the challenge of postulating humanistically preferable conditions, i.e., normative world models. In this regard their task is similar to that of clinical medicine, where diagnosis and prognosis are coupled with therapy based on a theory of normal functioning in the organism ("health"). When observations signal a deviation from the states defined in such theory, corrective strategies can be initiated by relating the anomalous conditions to the normal ones through deviation-reducing "therapeutic" processes. The analogy is clearly stated by Merton:[7]

First of all, certain functional requirements of the organism are established, requirements which must be satisfied if the organism is to survive, or to operate with some degree of effectiveness. Second, there is a concrete and detailed description of the arrangements (structures and processes) through which these requirements are typically met in "normal" cases. Third, if some of the typical mechanisms for meeting these requirements are destroyed, the observer is sensitized to the need for detecting compensating mechanisms (if any) which fulfill the necessary function. Fourth, and implicit in all that precedes, there is a detailed account of the structure for which the functional requirements hold, as well as a detailed account of the arrangements through which the function is fulfilled.

The therapeutic procedure, advocated by Merton in relation to a sociology of the middle range, is not new, and it also applies to the study of world order. Seneca observed that "between public madness and that treated by doctors the only difference is that the latter suffers from disease, the former from wrong opinions," and recently Falk has stressed this analogy as focal to efforts leading to a preferred world order.[8] Whether it is wrong opinions that today's world order system suffers from, or a more complex constellation of factors, it is clear that some of the mechanisms for meeting functional requirements in the global community are in danger of breaking down. Hence observers must be sensitized to the need for detecting compensating mechanisms. To do so they must have a detailed account of the structure for which the functional requirements hold, and of the various alternative arrangements through which the function can be fulfilled. The call is for a normative theory of world order, one which depicts an adequately functioning system. Such a theory would provide a reference for orienting our thinking and devising strategies to rectify real situations where some functional requirements are not met, and more may be left unsatisfied if present trends are allowed to develop.

## Framework for a General Systems Theory of World Order

(i)   *The Conceptual Fit of General Systems Theory*
    Social systems are not observables. Only selected aspects of them are empirically available, and these are given in the form of a wealth of complex data relating to individuals, groups, their psychologies, economies and ecologies, patterns of power and authority, social status, and so on. In themselves, the data do not generate models of social systems but serve only to validate or invalidate theoretical constructions. Theoretical constructions of social systems proceed by analogy with other phenomena that are more accessible to observation. The analogies of the past included naïve ones likening social systems to mechanisms on the one hand, and organisms on the other. Today, the analogies grow from the more fruitful terrain of a science of complex organization *per se*. Hereby the disciplinary bias inherent in attempts to transpose findings from one area of investigation to another without regard for intrinsic differences is overcome. Social systems are neither mechanisms nor organisms, but manifest some of the general principles of organization shared by both sophisticated varieties of servomechanisms and living organisms.
    Social systems are also not entirely different from other complexly organized phenomena. They are not so dissimilar to "natural" levels of organization that models and laws depicting the evolution of complex organization in physical and biological realms would be fully inapplicable to them. The assumption of the *sui generis* nature of society would make the use of general systems concepts an arbitrary imposition on

the phenomenon of human society. If the assumption is correct, social organization is more akin to the work of human engineers than to the workings of nature: not theories of evolution, but concepts of engineering—more specifically, social engineering—would apply.

This view of society underlies a philosophical movement based on the idea of a social contract, entered into by autonomous human beings in the light of their own sovereign wills. If society is the result of a contract between independent, rational agents, its characteristics are determined by the will of its members. This view is the outgrowth of a long tradition in which a state of nature is contrasted to civil society. In the former each man is for himself and not accountable to higher authority; in the latter he has surrendered his natural sovereignty in exchange for the security and goods of civilized life. The exchange is based on convention, and is the foundation of society. Society is thus radically distinguished from nature; social organization, and the organization of biological and ecological systems, for example, would have to be kept rigorously apart and even counterposed.

The *sui generis* concept of society suffers from the defect of abstract theory: it does not fully apply to the real phenomena. Real-world societies are not entirely based on human will and convention; they turn out to be highly complex systems often with counterintuitive multiple feedback loops between their components. As Lévi–Strauss points out, there is an important distinction between the conscious ideas its members entertain of a society and its actual "deep" structure; and Forrester has shown that the behavior of societies often frustrates the expectations of their members and proves that they are considerably more than the expression of their conscious wills and purposes.

Conventionalist and social contract conceptions of social phenomena sever the ties between theories of natural organization and theories of society. By contrast, the constellation of theories in the category known as Social Darwinism affirms such ties, and indeed overemphasizes them. Where conventionalist theorists claim that societies are unlike biological organisms in every important respect, Social Darwinists say that they are *like* organisms in all such respects. Both positions overshoot the mark. Societies are both different from, and analogous to, other forms of complex organization, and the differences and analogies can be specified. However, to hold that societies are but individuals "writ large" is unwarranted. Social Darwinists impute a number of basic biological attributes to societies, such as the need for growth (Ratzel's concept of *Lebensraum*), a predetermined sequence of aging (Spengler's view of cultures), and may even think of the planet as a living globe, with the continents comprising the primary organs of the superorganism (Ritter). Social Darwinism applied to the nation-state justifies aggression in the name of the struggle for survival which selects the fittest state, the one that can assure sufficient territorial possessions for itself. Such applications served Hitler's ideologues to further the cult of the Aryan German state in the name of science (e.g., Haushofer's *Geopolitik*).[9]

Theories cannot be blamed for the use to which they are put, and the failure of Social Darwinism is not that it was used by real and potential aggressors but that it indiscriminately reduces one level of organization to another. Nor is this approach extinct today: contemporary literature is still filled with examples of biological and ecological reasoning applied to social phenomena. For example, human interrelations are evaluated in terms of symbiosis, parasitism, niche-structures, and biological adaptation.

It is necessary to see both the differences and the similarities between social and biological forms of organization. We must neither transplant one empirical theory to another field, nor insist on entirely *ad hoc* theories. We can proceed from the generalized premise that systems of organized complexity arise in many sectors of reality; and these phenomena bear the marks of specific differentia as well as exhibit the invariants that result from common constraints of existence in this universe.* All processes of progressive evolution are processes of structuration supervening upon rich and enduring energy flows. Given a sufficiently rich flow over a sufficiently prolonged time-span, progressive structuration commences, limited by the laws of thermodynamics and supported by the cohesiveness of the possible systems of stable configuration.[10] Configurations exploiting the stability properties intrinsic to the flow have selective endurance over less stable configurations, and tend to dominate the flow pattern. The enduring configurations are further subjected to the fluxes in the flow and may hit upon metaconfigurations likewise endowed with a measure of stability.

This general evolutionary paradigm applies to all the important evolutionary processes, whether they involve the chemical build-up of the elements, the phylogenetic evolution of organic species, or the development of human sociocultural systems. The process obtains regardless of whether or not there is consciousness on the part of the entities it constitutes. In fact, consciousness arises but exceptionally, in our experience only at the intersection of the higher phases of biological with the lower phases of sociocultural evolution. The higher phases of the sociocultural process thereafter display the effects of consciousness, but their general characteristics continue to unfold analogously with the overall constraints of structuration. Hence when we compare parts of the process that involve consciousness with those that do not, we find that what changes is the specific character of the emerging struc-

---

* A review of the general systems hypotheses of evolution and systemic invariance is provided in the Appendix. Unless the reader is thoroughly familiar with these tenets of general systems theory, he would be well advised to peruse the Appendix at this point; it will aid in his understanding of the here proposed interpretation of general systems theory with respect to human societies.

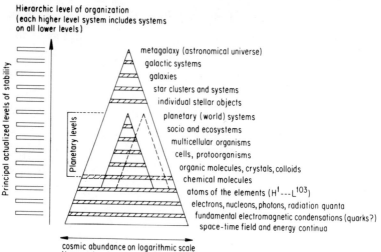

FIGURE I. A general map of the relationship of the principal levels of systems in the universe (outer triangle), on earth (inner triangle with solid sides), and possibly on other planetary surfaces (inner triangle with broken sides). Intervening levels and borderline systems are omitted for optimum simplicity and clarity. (Adapted from Ervin Laszlo, *Introduction to Systems Philosophy*, New York: Harper Torchbooks, 1973, 29.)

tures; but they continue to arise through mutual adaptation, competition, natural selection, and the symbiotic formation of superstructures. Whereas in the subconscious phases of the process energy transfers are the key agents of change, in phases where consciousness is already involved communication-flows (i.e., information superimposed on low-energy transfers) are the agency of interaction. The function of energy- and communication-flows is, however, quite similar as far as the overall character of the structuration process is concerned. As the human-communication theorist Klaus Krippendorf said, "any communication process, once initiated and maintained, leads to the genesis of social structure—whether or not such structure is anticipated or deemed desirable."[11]

The conclusion warranted by the systems theory of the evolution of complexity is that common processes of development characterize social and other forms of evolution, and that the products of these processes are therefore functionally similar. But differences in the manner in which the functions are performed exist and can be accounted for by reference to the level and phase at which they operate. Biological organisms evolve from the symbiotic behavior patterns of cellular and organ systems. Sociocultural systems arise from the mutually adaptive behavior patterns of human beings and their primary reproductive, social, economic, professional, cultural, and political groupings. Consequently social organization is neither a subspecies of biological organization nor something entirely *sui generis*. Societies are analogous to biological organisms in being complex open systems that maintain themselves in an environment characterized by variety with constraints. They differ from biological organisms in meeting their functional requirements through specifically societal, rather than specifically biological, regulative processes. Thus we find self-stabilization, self-organization, hierarchization, and irreducibility in societies as well as organisms, but they are expressed by different structures and produce qualitatively different phenomena.

(ii)  A *General Systems Interpretation of Sociocultural Evolution*

The general systems concepts and principles of evolution and systemic invariance provide a framework for the interpretation of the broad patterns of history. In this interpretation the investigated entities are formally or informally organized human groups, conceptualized as sociocultural systems. Such groups constitute open systems, i.e., have semipermeable boundaries that impose gradients on flows and represent discontinuities on the wider field of human social and cultural organization. Cohesiveness and continuity *within* the systems is higher, and rate of change lower, than in the relations *be-*

*tween* the systems. By such indicators, which apply to systems on biological and physical levels as well, it is possible to conceptually distinguish individual sociocultural systems, despite the many strands of relationships traversing the sociocultural field as a whole.

Thus isolated, basic systemic invariances are exhibited by sociocultural systems. We find that they have an ordered structure, the subject matter of treatises in social and cultural anthropology, sociology, economics, and the political sciences. They manifest properties which are irreducible to the properties of their individual members (although the personalities of leading figures in authoritarian systems are reflected in the economic and political structure of the systems). Furthermore, we find that sociocultural systems come into the class of self-stabilizing homeostatic systems; they achieve stability through the coordinated use of their effectors to counteract deviations from their established steady-states. In the political realm these functions are associated with conservatism and the maintenance of the status quo. In less formalized societies an entire array of societal mechanisms serves to stabilize existing patterns of life, including mores, customs, religions, myths, traditions, rituals, and so forth. In any complex sociocultural system there are sets of coexisting dynamics serving to maintain continuity by counterbalancing deviations from "law and order." There are institutional structures, value systems, as well as methods of persuasion and coercion, whereby the system seeks to reduce the effect of disturbance and return to its steady-state. This is a state characterized by the parameters of its constant contraints, i.e., the ideological, economic, and legal foundations of the community, state, or nation.

Self-organization is also evidenced in sociocultural systems. Historically, self-organization is the process of evolving more adapted and efficient sensing, decision-making, and effector structures, enabling the system to control its environment and grow. Growth can occur on one or several levels, including economic, cultural, military, and territorial growth. Self-organization combined with self-stabilization gives us the rich patterns of history. Here we see stability alternating with dynamic change, and can appreciate that the latter conduces to more complex and efficient organization in viable societies, but may also lead to the extinction of entire sociocultural systems if it is out of phase with the objective constraints of the environment.

In general, social structures are pattern-conserving, and technological innovations, as well as external disturbances, pattern transforming. Technology, with or without the challenge of external disturbance, tends to trigger growth through self-organization; social structures tend to capture the growth-curve at a viable level and stabilize the society on a new plateau of organization. The new level can be maintained if deviations forced on the system by external or internal perturbations do not exceed the organizational form's range of error correction. Beyond that range, positive feedback cycles take over, evolving the system toward new levels of organization, where it may or may not encounter appropriate forms of stability in the form of revised value systems, mores, reinterpreted or reformed traditions, and new juridical, economic, and political systems.

These processes have been described by the present writer under the heading of self-stabilizing "Cybernetics I" and self-organizing "Cybernetics II."[12] They correspond to the notions of "morphostasis" and "morphogenesis" propounded by Buckley.[13] Morphostasis refers to processes in complex system-environment exchanges that tend to preserve or *maintain* a system's given form, organization, or state. Morphogenesis refers to those processes which tend to elaborate or *change* a system's given form, structure, or state. Buckley emphasizes that homeostatic processes in organisms, and rituals in sociocultural systems, are examples of "morphostasis";

while biological evolution, learning, and societal development are examples of "morphogenesis." In his words, "the paradigm underlying the evolution of more and more complex adaptive systems begins with the fact of a potentially changing environment characterized by constrained variety and an adaptive system or organization whose persistence and elaboration to higher levels depends upon a successful mapping of some of the environmental variety and constraints into its own organization on at least a semipermanent basis."[14] Consequently sociocultural systems *qua* complex adaptive systems map into their internal structure the environmental variety relevant to their persistence, and preserve and propagate the successful mappings. The process results in the evolution of a limited set of progressively more complex sociocultural systems, satisfying, through increasingly sophisticated mechanisms, the requirements of adaptation to the relevant conditions in the environment.

Taylor has further developed this general systems model of sociocultural development, making explicit use of the concepts of Cybernetics I and Cybernetics II.[15] He points out that systems models have tended to be conceptualized "horizontally," i.e., either as a single sociopolitical system, or else as a set of transacting systems in a similar state of development. But we still have to account for the "vertical" shifts of societal organization to explain the historical progression from relatively simple and homogeneous societies to complex and heterogeneous ones. Thus the negative feedback model of functionalist sociology and systems-oriented political theory has to be supplemented with a model that has both negative and positive feedbacks—morphostasis as well as morphogenesis. Taylor's model accounts for both systemic self-stabilization within a given level of societal organization and integration, and systemic transformation from level to level.

Negative feedback (morphostatic) processes dominate when innovation in a society is at a low ebb and the society is primarily devoted to coping with its environmental contingencies through the existing norms and codes of organized behavior. Animal societies rely primarily on genetically coded mechanisms of societal organization (although some higher primates show definite traces of specifying these codes through acquired, socially communicated habits and practices); and primitive man, inasmuch as he relies more on his instincts than on his knowledge for survival, likewise operates within a societal dynamics that is genetically stabilized through biological inheritance. Its progress is dependent on mutations in the genotype, rather than on changes in the empirically acquired culture. With the appearance of toolmaking abilities in man, such *biologically* adaptive stabilizing mechanisms give place to *culturally* adaptive modes. These are open to relatively rapid evolution, relying not on genetically but on empirically transmitted information. Cultural evolution, based on the ability to make tools, and create and communicate new knowledge, brings with it an improved control capability over the environment. It is encoded in a new societal structure, representing a distinct level above that of the instinctual, mainly ritualistic one. Technology—in the broad sense where it includes all forms of purposive human control over the natural environment—introduces a positive feedback element in the development of sociocultural systems: it changes the man–environment relation and prompts the appearance of new forms of societal organization. But all newly emerged forms of societal organization evolve conservative elements, providing for their own continuity and stability. These are the emerging institutions, values, mores, and their accompanying rituals, world views, religions and, at a more sophisticated stage, the established legal and political structures.

It thus appears that the societal technics just described function to stabilize sociocultural systems at their mature level of organization, and the material technics, or environmental technologies, destabilize systems and move them toward new levels of organization.[16] The former process incorporates a dominant negative feedback element and is an instance of Cybernetics I; the latter contains a dominant positive feedback mode and represents Cybernetics II.

Cybernetics I occurs both at primitive levels of societal existence, where such technologies as exist are mainly biologically coded and have little potential for inducing rapid changes in organization, and at mature stages in the development of societies where the culturally transmitted technologies have reached the limits of their operational effectiveness. By contrast, Cybernetics II operates whenever new technologies are evolved in a sociocultural system. Taylor gives as examples the control of fire and the invention of progressively more sophisticated and efficient tools by the Eskimos. Thanks to the development of a highly specialized technology, they were able to survive beyond the timberline and maintain a viable symbiosis with a low-energy physical environment. However, the constraints of the environment set upper limits on the development of their technology, and Eskimo societies stabilized at a well-defined level of societal organization, reinforced by traditions, values, mores, and habits. In other, more favorable environments technologies could evolve further, and societies stabilized at higher organizational levels. For example, the "Neolithic Revolution" of agriculture and the domestication of animals elicited new settlement patterns, new forms of societal organization, more complex division of labor, and the growth of the human population. However, in some areas the environment imposed limits on this technological development too, and forced the systems to stabilize at the upper bounds of their capacities. This was the case at Jericho and Jarmo, where the scarcity of water supplies set strict limits on the development of agriculture and the use of domestic animals.

Where the environment was still more favorable, new technologies prompted further evolution in patterns of social organization. The transplanting of farming technics to the rich bottomlands of the Nile, Tigris–Euphrates, Indus, and Huang-ho made possible a great increase in agricultural productivity and could support a vastly increased population. This in turn called for the evolution of more complex forms of societal organization, with increasingly large groups of people functioning in an administrative and regulative, rather than in a directly productive capacity. Towns arose with progressively sophisticated administrative and governmental structures. With them we witness the move to the next major level of sociocultural organization, where urban civilizations control entire river valleys, equipped with mature technologies and well-defined rules of social behavior.

Sociocultural systems moved beyond this stage of organization too, when further refinements of their environmental control capabilities enabled them to control vaster territories —less hospitable lands, and the seas. Thus arose the great agricultural and maritime civilizations of the Middle Ages. Their relatively stable patterns were shattered with the technological spin-offs of modern science: the advent of industrial civilization. We are now moving toward a global industrial and post-industrial civilization made possible through the invention of instantaneous global communication networks, worldwide trade facilitated by fast transport technologies, and increasing interdependence among the established political, military, economic, and ecologic structures.

The evolution of sociocultural systems exhibits a growth pattern characterized by progressive hierarchization. Sociocultural evolution has proceeded by building dynamically stable systems through the mutual adaptation of existing systems, and then adapting the thus formed larger systems with similar systems in their environment to form still more inclusive units. Primitive societies, such as clans and tribes, were integrated into village structures with the advent of agricul-

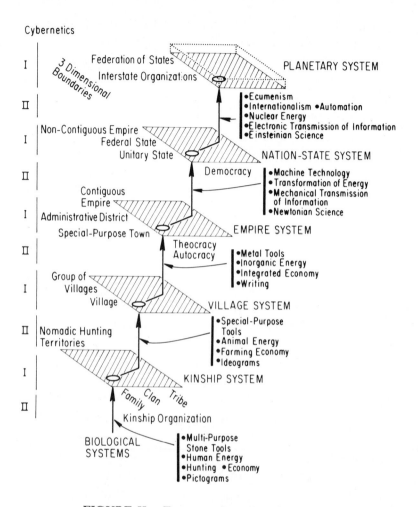

FIGURE II.  Emergent Geopolitical Systems.

ture and a sedentary mode of life; villages were in turn integrated with one another to form locally cohesive cultures. In some regions city-states arose; in others a more diffuse organization has emerged, bound by a common language, shared values, and economic and political interdependence. Already in classical times, the more powerful units could impose their rule on the weaker ones and form empires. The rise of sea powers and international trade in the Middle Ages brought about the phenomenon of mercantilism and the establishment of colonial regimes. With it evolved the European concept of the nation-state as a sovereign entity. In this century colonialism suffered a demise and the thereby liberated peoples entered on the scene as nation-states endowed with the legal rights of sovereignty. Since 1945 the number of such actors has more than doubled. Hence in the last decades the thrust toward the formation of progressively larger geopolitical units has been reversed. Although integration proceeds in all functional respects—in the world economy, culture, communication, mobility, military bloc formation, and multinational corporate structure—it is halted in the political area on the level of the seventeenth-century concept of sovereign nation-states. Attempts to weld larger regional polities have so far failed—the federation of European states still awaits realization, and even the United Arab Republic, though bonded by strong common motivations focused by the presence of Israel, has shattered. Portugal remains virtually the sole empire, though an insignificant one; the political organization of the rest of the world, however heterogeneous it may be, is along the lines of the "sovereign equality" of states. Even participation in the United Nations, the only universal political organization, is premised on this recalcitrant and currently totally inadequate concept.

## Norms for a Future World Order

The application of the basic concepts of general systems theory to the patterns of development in sociocultural systems suggests a "grand view" of history, reminiscent of Spengler and Toynbee. A general theory of the evolution of sociocultural systems can indeed be produced on the general systems matrix,[17] but it is not the purpose of this study to do so. Rather, the application of general systems concepts to the sociocultural sphere is to provide us with normative reference points for envisaging a functional and humanistic world order and devising the strategies capable of leading to its realization.

Periods of rapid change produce so many issues calling for resolution that little time and energy is left to consider their meaning and long-term consequences. Therefore the most serious problem becomes, as Kissinger says, the need to acquire a sufficiently wide perspective so that the present does not overwhelm the future.[18] The conceptual synthesis founded on the principles of general systems theory offers a framework for acquiring such a perspective. It helps us to penetrate the meaning and the consequences of current developments, and to set our sights, so that the present will not overwhelm the future. But the view offered by this approach is not narrowly deterministic. Despite the elucidation of the grand patterns of history, we are not left in the position of the helpless spectator, or of the involved but equally helpless cog in the machinery, perceiving the advance of history but unable to influence its path. The lessons of a perspective sufficiently wide to safeguard the future from the preoccupations of the present are normative but not deterministic. They let us recognize that cosmic history would not be shaken in its foundations were the human species to disappear from earth, or undergo a cataclysmic transition to some more enduring form of world order.

But the lessons of history, viewed as the evolution of complexity in the societal realm, tell us that sociocultural systems to be stable must have the necessary regulative and adaptive capacities, and that if they are to be humanistic in addition, they must focus their self-regulated steady-states on patterns of equitable distribution of the basic resources of satisfactory human existence. We may not be able to tell whether any given system will realize such conditions, at least not with certainty, but we can tell what the conditions are and what is involved in attaining them. Having a normative model of societal organization at hand, we can go beyond the sterile alternatives of historical determinism or indeterminism, and purposively intervene in the development of our systems, in the effort to render them more functional and humanly satisfying. Having such a model at our command is especially important today, at a time when the pace of evolution is faster by several magnitudes than it has ever been before. Technological and societal innovations can be produced, communicated, and exploited in record-breaking times, using modern electronic communication media, technological hardware, and sociopolitical software. Already within our lifetime, the vast acceleration of sociocultural development could inflict irreversible harm on humanity. But the same technologies which make for accelerated development can also be used for steering the processes. For effective steering, however, we need realistic norms of humanistic and functional organization.

The systems concept of the evolution of complexity, applied to sociocultural systems, provides us with two normative points of reference in designing our strategies for the future. The first point is that if we are to achieve optimum humanistic conditions of existence, our sociocultural systems must not continue to grow in those functional respects which depress the planet's potentials for satisfying high standards of life. The second point of reference is that in the area of political organization we still have a long way to grow, before we catch up with the (apparent) limits to growth already encountered in some of the functional areas.

(I) What are the humanistic conditions of existence for mankind as a whole? To define such conditions we must know what man truly needs to fulfill himself, and achieve the condition variously referred to as self-actualization, contentment, or happiness. Human needs must however be separated from human wants. And we must distinguish between needs that can be realistically satisfied on this planet for all people, and needs that presuppose elitism and injustice.

Human beings are self-maintaining open systems, drawing from their environment all the energies and information necessary for their survival and reproduction. Obviously, their needs are for an environment in which these energies and information are available. But survival needs do not exhaust the spectrum of human needs. Beyond physical survival man needs social contact, and satisfaction of his desire to know and his thirst for beauty and enjoyment. To reduce man to bare survival is to frustrate many of his satisfiable needs.

However, not everything people want is a need. Many wants are directly harmful, for the individual who wants them, those around him, or for all concerned. The old-fashioned recipe of laissez faire individual enterprise economy, "Give people what they want," is misleading and unrealistic. People cannot get all they want, even if they often want all they can get. There are constraints inherent in the physical universe which must be respected (nobody can travel faster than light or ignore gravity), and there are many more constraints inherent in social organization (if resources are finite, the laws of distribution prevent anyone from getting all there is—and in many cases, all that he wants). There are further restrictions associated with particular modes of social organization: laws regulating behavior, commerce, industry, travel, the acquisition of wealth and position, and so on.

Genuine needs form a subset of all the things that can be obtained without harm in an optimal form of social organization. Whenever such things cannot be had by all members of a society because of deficient social organization, social conditions are less than optimally humanistic. They should be reformed according to the logic of humanism.

Man as an open system interacts with his environment, and

that environment is predominantly structured by his society. If he is not to frustrate himself and those around him, his satisfactions must not reduce the humanism of his society, i.e., the general patterns of need-fulfillments. If persons have a right to need-fulfillment, this right entails that their fulfillments do not interfere with the similar fulfillments of those around them. Hence society can recognize as a genuine need only those desires for fulfillment which harm neither the individual nor transcend the constraints inherent in social organization.

The individually and socially permissible needs fall into a hierarchic sequence where the lower fulfillments are preconditions of the higher ones. Several such need-categories have been investigated (e.g., by Piaget, Maslow, Bruner, Koestler) and some common features have come to light. These can be grasped in relation to the general concepts of physiological (survival) needs and psychological (sociocultural) needs. In an inclusive categorization, based on Maslow's investigations,[19] the hierarchy shapes up as follows:

Physiological needs (food, air, water, behavioral space, etc.)
Safety needs (protection from weather, other species, and other humans)
Belongingness and love needs (family and social group membership)
Esteem needs (having the respect of oneself and his/her peers in society)
Self-actualization needs (fulfilling one's potentials in his/her private and public capacities)
Cognitive needs (understanding one's relations to society and comprehending order in nature and the cosmos)
Aesthetic needs (perceiving beauty and order in experience)

The levels of human experience corresponding to these needs move from the experience of the behavioral space through time with its essential elements capable of sustaining life, to experiences that refer to others in society, reaching ultimately "peak-experiences" where a creative integration of all one's knowledge of self and others mediates a new level of meaning and fulfillment.

It is evident that social organization cannot be the sufficient condition of all such experiences, but for many, it can be the necessary condition. Since the Neolithic Age, and even before, physiological needs have been fulfilled through social cooperation with typical patterns of access to and distribution of the basic necessities of life. Some of these were equally accessible to all, such as water in early times (except in dry zones), and air until recently. Today even these basic necessities are mediated by social organization, which pollutes air, forces water into conduits, and has citizens pay for the privilege of access through air purification systems and water taps. Food is available as a market commodity, and has become an extension of the economy. Safety needs are likewise socially fulfilled (insofar as they may be fulfilled at all). Police forces attempt to protect individual citizens from acts of personal aggression, and one wonders what structures exist to protect people from acts of collective aggression, committed by governments in the name of their nation-states.

Belongingness and love needs are mediated by society in affording a framework for encounters and sustained social as well as sexual relations. Social organization can impose various degrees of socialization and alienation on its members, conducing toward contentment with interpersonal relations on the satisfying end of the spectrum, and loneliness and frustration on the dissatisfying end. Esteem needs are likewise dependent on social organization for satisfaction, functioning not as their sufficient, but in most cases as their necessary condition. Few people can achieve sufficient self-esteem to be able to disregard the esteem of others, and esteem by others is mediated through an organizational structure in which the individual figures as a role-carrier.

Self-actualization is at least conditioned by social organization. The ability to unfold one's capacities depends on a constructive environment in which latent potentials for love, belongingness, esteem, knowledge, aesthetic enjoyment, and the integration of all in peak-experiences, can grow to fruition. The basic features of such an environment are socially determined. While individuals can self-actualize in relatively poor environments as well as fail to do so in rich ones, the chances of self-actualization are increased by the structure of their milieu—which in turn is an effect of social organization. Aesthetic needs are also greatly contingent on social conditions. Ghetto areas are notably lacking in aesthetic stimulation (except perhaps for the romantic and the visionary), while a distinct characteristic of elevated social position is the attempt to restructure the environment in accordance with dominant aesthetic sensibilities—surround oneself with what one considers not merely useful, but also pleasing, beautiful, and intrinsically excellent. Here too, the pattern of social organization functions as a conditioning factor, determining the probability, if not the individual occurrence, of aesthetic satisfactions.

Peak-experiences are the most introverted, and hence removed from societal conditions. Yet it is difficult to achieve such an experience when one is hungry, tired, lonely, rejected, frustrated, puzzled, and surrounded by squalor.

If social organization is to be humanistic, it must respond to some such categories of needs, satisfying them in a hierarchic sequence. It must assure physiological satisfactions as a basis; provide security in the form of protection from individually or collectively designed harm; offer a context for social interaction where individuals can find self-esteem and earn the esteem of others; provide in addition a well-structured learning environment which permits individuals to perceive the meaning of life, nature, and society; and assure, last but not least, an environment capable of inspiring feelings of beauty and significance.

These are the conditions of humanism which social organization is to fulfill. Only an ideal society could do so with perfection. In the real world we must expect trade-offs. In a well-functioning society they involve the higher needs; they become indicative of serious deficiencies when they approach the lower ones. At the least, physiological, safety, belongingness and esteem needs must be satisfiable. Above that we move from the tolerable to the excellent and have more freedom in effecting compromises.

Hitherto, societal growth (measured by territory, wealth, population-size, military power, ideological influence) did (or was believed to) increase amenities that we could assess as conditions of need-fulfillment. With continued growth in some areas, there are strong indications that the chances of need-fulfillment will be diminished, i.e., that conditions of life will become less, rather than more, humanistic. The problem facing our generation is to level off growth wherever further growth stifles needs rather than satisfies them. If growth is left unchecked, the hierarchy of needs will be progressively frustrated—removing, in the end, the very conditions of survival.

A global steady-state is an inevitable condition of long-term survival on this planet. As Boulding once remarked, anyone who believes that exponential growth can continue indefinitely in a finite world is either a madman or an economist. In a finite world, where the laws of the conservation of mass and energy hold, the economy can only continue to grow if there are unending advances in recycling technologies and, since materials from which energy is drawn cannot be recycled, also parallel advances in expandable sources of energy. And only if these technologies progress fast enough to prevent the accumulation of residuals can economic growth be sustained. Population growth comes up against limitations of habitable space and food and water supplies. Even if living near subsistance level, much as Stone Age man did, there are upper bounds for the population sustainable on this planet. If some or all of the population depends on higher technological standards of living, then economic growth must be correlated with population growth, and we face both problems simultaneously.

However, the concept of a global steady-state need not be the dismal one which makes most economists react with horror. It calls neither for immediately effective Zero Economic Growth (ZEG) nor Zero Population Growth (ZPG). The ills of leveling off in these areas at present, and then keeping to that arbitrary level, are well known: they involve an unhealthy age distribution of the population, stagnation in industrial societies, and the full loss of the social and psychological momentum which sustained Western-type civilization over the past two hundred years. While that kind of growth cannot be continued, a slow-down process could begin which can conduce toward a multivariable steady-state, where some parameters are kept constant, others decrease, and some develop. We may have, for example, population growth in some regions and stability in others, adding up to a modest global population growth-rate. It may be correlated with a capital stock likewise increasing, decreasing, or remaining constant in different sectors and at different rates. Even where capital stock is stable, its composition may change, having a smaller output of nonrecyclable goods but a larger average life expectancy, and a larger output of services and service-oriented products. We might ultimately have a constant capital stock in the world economy with less environmental load, coupled with a smaller population which would thus enjoy a greater per capita standard of life. Various subsystem accommodations jointly yield an overall state which has the characteristic of a multivariable steady-state. Such a state does not present the dismal picture of a stagnating, motivationless society. Those who foresee such a condition equate an arbitrarily enforced unilateral stationary state with a dynamic, multivariable steady-state. (Nevertheless, the term "steady" has static connotations, and in later chapters we shall prefer to speak of "*optimum*-states" instead.)

Will there be ennui and loss of motivation in a steady ("optimum")-state society? We cannot see into the future, but can answer with confidence that there *need not be*. Innovation and creativity are enduring elements of human societies, just as they are permanent features in the evolution of all complex systems. The development of stabilizing capability in a system does not mean the withering of such elements, only their reorientation. Growth without limit is counterfunctional, and when it is realized to be that, motivation ceases to support such growth and seeks other pathways of activity. An enduring ideal in the evolution of sociocultural systems is the search for patterns of social organization capable of satisfying human needs on all levels of the need-hierarchy. When doing so for a powerful elite is premised on frustrating the higher need-fulfillments of the rest, societal progress is temporarily halted. When the administration of the societal mechanisms becomes bureaucratized and unresponsive to innovation, progress likewise comes to a stop. There are many cases of regress, of descending to stable plateaus of organization which offer less fulfillment to many, or more selective fulfillments to different strata, than do previous organizational forms. But behind every major transformation of social order there is the ideal to increase the level of human satisfaction for a great portion of the population. Such an ideal may lie constrained during periods of elitism and autocracy and be frozen into immobility by bureaucracies. But it is never totally extinguished, except as a sign of the final decay of the culture.

In the past two centuries, growth in the area of the economy constituted the main ideal for Western civilization, and produced undreamt-of power over the natural environment as well as triggered a worldwide population explosion. Humanity need not remain locked into this growth-ideology when it becomes dysfunctional. The tasks of increasing the adaptability of social organization to the needs of sociocultural human beings offer multiple possibilities for creativity and innovation. Our sociocultural systems can grow toward a level of stable organization where functionality is combined with humanism. The real goal ahead is to find this plateau of organization, and center human motivation toward attaining and maintaining it.

(II) Transforming our growth-oriented societies into a humanistic and self-regulative global community poses a number of problems in the realm of purposive guidance. The fact is that although the functional aspects of human systems grew to global dimensions, the growth of decision-making structures capable of coordinating and guiding development has been arrested at the level of nation-states. World politics operates on the premise that nation-states are the highest functional units of political decision-making. This is the "logic of Westphalia": the concept of the role and status of nation-states postulated in the Peace of Westphalia that, in 1648, brought the Thirty Years War to an end.[20] This logic endows the nation-state with ultimate, quasi-metaphysical independence. In its light the nation-state is (i) sovereign, i.e., knows no secular authority higher than itself, and (ii) the full possessor and controller of its geographical territory and the population living there. A sovereign nation-state can enter into voluntary arrangements, such as treaties, with other nation-states to regulate its external relations. But all parties to international treaties are sovereign and equal, and acknowledge no higher authority or the right to greater influence by reasons of wealth, power, or size. The essential characteristics of nation-states thus include a defined territory, a permanent population, a government acting solely in their interest, and a capacity to voluntarily enter into external relations. Although the logic of states was evolved already in 1648, and since then world history has known its perhaps most explosive period of development, it is still dominant on today's political scene. It also underlies the United Nations Charter (Article 2[1]), where all member states are given the status of "sovereign equality" independently of existing ties of interdependence, and of differences in power, wealth, prestige, territory, education, culture, and population.

This arbitrary freezing of the geopolitical growth process on the nation-state level is inherently dangerous, given the transcendence of that level in all other respects. Multinational corporations spread to all parts of the world, regardless of political, and even of ideological boundaries (several large corporations now operate plants and branch offices in the socialist-bloc countries including the Soviet Union); supranational functional organizations develop at a rapid pace and operate in the areas of health, environmental protection, finance, ocean and space use, disaster relief, peace-keeping, and resource conservation; intergovernmental and nongovernmental international organizations multiply in number at an astonishing pace; cultural exchange intensifies between spatially contiguous as well as removed peoples; the flow of information is potentially global and is restricted only by the will of national governments; and the flow of people across continents likewise increases, for business as well as for recreation. Only national governments continue to act as if the units they controlled had sovereign independence and sovereign equality.

The dangers associated with statist logic are well known, and a brief summary will suffice to recall the principal points. As long as nation-states equate their sovereign interests with economic growth, international conflict will be inevitable. This results from several factors, such as the finiteness of basic raw material and energy resources as well as of space, conflicting ideologies with imperialistic ambitions, and existing disparities in wealth and power.

For example, world oil supplies are finite and may be depleted in the foreseeable future. Until national industries can develop and exploit other sources of energy, they will be in competition for the existing supplies. The needs of the advanced industrial nations are not matched by the needs of the oil-rich nations, however. The United States' oil requirements vastly exceed the developmental needs of the oil-producing Arab states: Saudi Arabia estimates that it need not sell more than 8 million barrels a day to finance its internal development, and Kuwait cannot spend more than the revenues from 3 million barrels. Yet oil revenues for Saudi Arabia could reach $15 billion in 1974. Since the Saudis do not need more than $3 billion, they can accumulate vast reserves: as much as $100 billion by the late 1970s. This could make Saudi Arabia the wealthiest nation in the world, wealthier, in terms of reserves, than the United States, Western Europe, and Japan combined.

In a world balanced at the edge of great-power competition, the emergence of super-rich small nations, holding vital resources at their command, is a dangerous phenomenon. With inflation plaguing most of the Western world's great economies, internal dissension in the European Community as well as among the Communist nations, and limits to expansion in Japan coupled with the unstable situation in the Middle East, unparalleled wealth and discretionary power in the hands of a few Arab leaders could lead to progressive tensions and eventually an armed showdown.

And for now, the rich nations continue to get richer and the poor to get poorer. Disparity in wealth between nations now exceeds the fantastic ratio of 40:1; and half of the world's population exists at or below the poverty line. Millions die every year of malnutrition. Similar inequalities obtain in other areas measured by economic indicators: energy consumption, food production, usage of raw materials, pollution generation, population growth and per capita income.

The perceived economic interests of nations dictate measures that are directly at odds. In view of the limitations of basic economic resources, the wealthy nations seek to maintain the differences. The poor nations strive toward equalization. Equalization can occur, however, only by reducing the GNP of the wealthy nations concurrently with increasing that of the poor ones. Economic dedevelopment is not currently contemplated by the wealthy nations, most of which may be ready to defend their economies with arms. They spend a staggering proportion of their wealth on defense, attempting to maintain their dominance through a balance of great powers. Statist logic entails reliance on self-defense, and self-defense entails maintaining a balance of power among the superpowers. Thanks to the destructive potential of the nuclear arsenals of the great powers, major wars have so far been avoided. But limited conflicts are sustained on the outskirts of the major blocs, and opposing ideologies are merely contained, not harmonized. Peace-keeping relies on the imagery of balance and equilibrium, but sovereign national interest, which for the major powers means mainly interest in continued economic growth, remains the ultimate motivation of action and justification of decision. Thus war in the national interest is always a possibility, and can always be justified. The aggressor may deny imperialist intent and define war as legitimate self-defense, as aid to a threatened ally, or as a step necessary to reestablish balance for enduring peace. Any nation is free to exempt itself from military alignments or armament limitation treaties if it perceives this exemption to be dictated by its sovereign interests. France can continue testing its nuclear weapon systems despite the test-ban treaty respected by both the Soviet Union and the United States, and notwithstanding decisions by the International Court of Justice.

Competition for economic growth leads to conflicts, and conflicts can lead to war. Limited war can lead to wider involvements, and conventional war can transform into nuclear warfare. As long as regulation in the world system is vested in national governments, and national governments strive to maximize their sovereign national interests defined in terms of wealth and power, the global situation remains highly unstable. If a more stable and equitable world order is to be striven for, we must envisage normative models of world order where the factors that destabilize the contemporary world are removed, and new, more adequate regulative capacities are evolved. Such a normative model of world order may be reconstituted on the basis of the general systems conception of sociocultural evolution and functioning.

In this conception, the contemporary world order appears unstable because of a seriously one-sided pattern of development. The system is stressed by the excessive development of its material technics (the various technologies of environmental control and resource use) vis-à-vis the development of its societal technics (the technologies of social organization and control). Since reversing twentieth-century technologies to the level of earlier centuries appears unrealistic, there is no other choice but to lift the level of societal technics to a corresponding level. This means, in fact, the globalization of the decision-making organization and control processes which are currently vested in national governments. Only if the phase-relations of world-systemic growth are straightened out can we look forward to a dynamically stable world system—one that maintains the constancies essential to a satisfactory existence for the human population. As long as world systemic growth is out-of-phase, the next plateau of societal organization that offers stability coupled with humanistic conditions is not attained; and world order remains prey to instabilities that may lead to a drastic deterioration in the global quality of life.

Clearly, our interests lie with reaching the next plateau of stable and humanistic world order. This suggests the need for a world authority, to transform competition and incoordination on the international level into collaboration and controlled development. But what form should such world authority take? World government advocates perceive the need for a global political structure that is analogous to national governments. The rationale for world government may point to the state of *an-archy* that prevails in the field of international relations and the need to subject it to some first cause or principle (*arche*). Or the reasoning may espouse the distinction between the state of nature and civil society, and conclude with the need for more "civility" on the global level.

One variant of this reasoning may follow Hobbesian lines. Hobbes argued (e.g., in the *Leviathan*) that all men by nature pursue the ends of individual gain. But since the goods they desire are scarce, not all men's desires can be satisfied. Hence in the "state of nature" men are at war with one another to assure access to the goods they desire. But since not all men are equally strong, there is no equitable distribution of the stock of resources; the mightiest obtain the largest share and the weakest nothing. War is the logical condition in the state of nature; self-restraint and self-denial are not only not practiced—they are actually foolish. For some persons would exploit the self-sacrifice even of a majority, and the resulting inequalities would set the norms of social intercourse. Consequently the only solution, Hobbes said, is to erect a common power structure dominating all social relations and compelling people to accept laws founded on reason. The principal such law is that one may never exercise one's own rights in a way that compromises the rights of others. The disparity between this rational concept of political order and the misery of the state of nature will draw men toward the former. The structure envisaged by Hobbes was personified by the sovereign. To him all men voluntarily surrender their individual sovereignty in exchange for the common order based on the rational concept. Autocracy by consent is the only solution to the problem posed by the excess of demands over supplies.

The very same argument that led Hobbes to envisage the

sovereign as the head of the people may be used to justify the concept of world sovereign. International relations today bear striking resemblance to the "state of nature" described by Hobbes. The attraction of a rational concept of surrendered national sovereignty in exchange for collective security and shared wealth attracts the contemporary advocates of world government, as Hobbes said individual men would be attracted by the concept of a rational political order on the national. scale.

But the Hobbesian reasoning involves the fallacy of all social-contract–based theories of civil society: it assumes that men can constitute a political society at will, depending only on their agreement on the principles. Large political units are not made, however, but grow; they grow out of societal processes where the purposes and motivations of the participating systems are gradually harmonized, and prove amenable to coordination and control by a governing body. Governmental frameworks and principles can be designed in the absence of such conditions, but they will either remain on the drawing boards of the social engineers, or be implemented only by coercion. Ideas fuel processes of social change, but become ripe for application when those processes have done their work. History testifies to this even in its periods of great revolutions, such as the French and the Russian. As long as the world's real societal processes involve decision-making by the heads of nation-states, and such decision-making does not create worldwide trauma, ideas of world government by well-meaning but politically powerless individuals remain utopian. To strive toward a world authority with sufficient capacity to regulate critical trends and processes, we must first create the conditions which elicit the relevance of our theoretic conceptions. Then we must measure these conceptions against the real possibilities of implementation.

When we face the problem of implementation in any time-frame of less than a hundred years hence, i.e., within a reasonably foreseeable period, we shall have solid reasons for exchanging visions of world government for more modest and more realistic conceptions. Societal processes are unlikely to permit the implementation of world government ideas in the foreseeable future. The ideas we presently entertain are modeled on the pattern of national governments and require that the entire population of the world constitute a manageable set of people and institutions, not exceeding in diversity and complexity the domestic conditions of average-size nations. Even the larger of the contemporary nations prove to be too complex for smooth processes of government by existing principles. In the U.S. and the U.S.S.R., for example, there is too much heterogeneity to permit governance by a single political philosophy without grievances and the arbitrary enforcement of a partially foreign sense of law and order. Yet diversity on the global level is incomparably richer still. If a kind of world government would head it which we now know from national political experience, it would almost certainly need to exercise highly coercive policies to stay in power. No matter which of the contemporary political philosophies and ideologies we envisage for adoption by a world government, it would be sure to be perceived as arbitrary, and even downright wrong, by at least one-third of the world's population. A simple transposition of national governmental principles to the global level is mistaken, even if the global problems we face today are similar to those which led Hobbes to envisage his national sovereign.

The question is, then, what kind of a political system can be responsive to current global needs without exercising arbitrary coercion in carrying out its mandate? It is clear that whatever system we postulate, it must permit diversity without letting it disrupt cohesion and coordination, and must govern in the functional sense of steering processes away from inherently dangerous paths rather than in the traditional sense of exercising power and authority for the sake of their self-perpetuation. To highlight the differences between the functional global steering process and the global transplant of the national government concept, we shall speak of a "central guidance system" rather than of "world government." A central guidance system, unlike a more traditional form of world government, is capable of exercising a measure of control over critical global processes without having to deny different political-ideological systems the right of existence. It can recognize that entirely different ideological and political structures may be functionally equivalent as regards their effects on the relevant global conditions. A socialist technology pollutes neither more nor less than a capitalist one, nor does it differ in its potential to harvest food and natural resources. The impact of politically organized systems on the international environment differs according to the level of actualized technological potential, not the principles by which that potential is actualized. Hence it is unnecessary to impose common organizing principles on politically constituted entities— it is sufficient to prevent them from stressing the carrying capacity of the global environment beyond levels where human qualities of life suffer irreversible damage.*

Even the possibility of implementing such a limited global regulative capability may encounter scepticism. If present values and objectives do not change, collaboration will not replace competition, and growth will continue wherever it can, limited only by natural constraints. These views represent the doomsday theories of the future, succinctly dubbed by Boulding the "dismal theorem."[21] If the only check to growth is starvation and misery, the population will grow until it is miserable and starves. Its corollary is the "utterly dismal theorem" according to which any improvement, in productivity, for instance, has only temporary benefits and ultimately creates a larger population living in starvation and

---

* Chapter 6 develops the concept of a central guidance system and suggests a blueprint for its operation.

misery. Fortunately, the dismal theory has a cheerful lemma: if things other than starvation and misery can check economic and population growth, then population does not have to grow until it is miserable and starves, but can reach a steady-state at a more humane level.

The "other things" that can check growth in the economy and population of human societies all come under the general category of values and world views. If these can change in time, starvation and misery can be avoided through preventive reorientations. Values govern the formation of popular consensus, and popular consensus influences practical politics. Ultimately, the long-term goals of a society determine whether or not it can *prevent* trauma, or is swayed only by the "heavy hand of fate."

If a global regulatory organization is to be implemented within foreseeable time to perform the essential stabilizing functions, it requires the creation of a broad basis of popular consensus, penetrating upwards through national societies through changing decision-making structures. The values of today are inadequate to handle the constraints of tomorrow; but today's values, fortunately, are changeable. Soon we shall all be living in a spaceship almost as vulnerable and in need of purposive guidance as today's airplanes. As we need aviation control and security mechanisms today to enjoy a safe and comfortable flight, so we shall need control and regulatory mechanisms tomorrow to enjoy a safe and comfortable existence. People show surprising understanding for the inconvenience of security checks and accident-prevention measures connected with aviation, conscious of the dangers of doing otherwise. We may expect that they will show similar comprehension for the necessary constraints of global self-regulation, when they become conscious of the dismal alternatives.

The basic conclusions that emerge from such considerations are these. First, we must limit our concepts of a normative world order to what is feasible to accomplish within a reasonable time-frame. This means abandoning dreams of world government and restricting our plans to the creation of a universal functional organization with just sufficient power and authority to regulate critical decisions concerning global security, economy, ecology, and population growth, removing these matters from the discretion of national governments operating on the principle of individual sovereignty. Second, we must recognize that even a limited form of functional guidance cannot be implemented without consciously speeding up the processes of societal reorganization and the transformation of values and world views. This in turn points to the need for dealing with means in addition to ends; with strategies as well as objectives.

The preceding chapters, composing Part One of the present book, have been devoted mainly to providing the theoretical validation for purposive activism aimed at the creation of a more stable and humanistic world order. It sought to expose general patterns of sociocultural development that point toward the alternatives of attaining matching levels of material and societal technics, or facing the decadence and dissolution of societies and cultures. As members of the emerging global society and culture of the late twentieth century, we are committed to seeking the new forms of societal organization which enable mankind to enter the era of global existence without trauma and the decimation of our numbers. The systems approach suggests the cure, as well as diagnoses the illness, of mankind's present condition.

Part Two is devoted to a program of therapy. Based on a conception of what is wrong, it outlines a possible way of righting it. Thus we move from the discussion of ends to the scrutiny of means; from the systems approach to a preferred world order to the strategies designed to bring it about.

# PART TWO

■

*A Strategy for*
*the Future*

# 3

# THE INDIVIDUAL AND WORLD ORDER: THE STRATEGY OF POPULAR INVOLVEMENT

Strategies for the future need not be idle exercises in utopian thinking. Given our needs as well as our capabilities, if we can envisage a desirable and realistically attainable world order, we can also devise strategies for achieving it.

The vision of the future world order outlined in Part One is neutral with respect to many specific ideologic-political proposals. It insists merely on achieving the general norms derived from the systems theoretical study of world order: in-phase development toward a dynamically stable and humanly satisfying enduring world system. The desirable world order is one that overcomes the instabilities and dangers associated with the current out-of-phase growth of material and societal technologies and their control capacities, and evolves the means whereby a high-quality pattern of life can be assured for the entire, still rapidly increasing human population.

Strategies of this kind are usually addressed to elites. It is assumed that governmental leaders can manage their populations to achieve whatever objectives can be reasonably postulated. However, by the very nature of our current problems, this option becomes secondary. National governments acting to maximize the wealth and power of independent states face inevitable conflicts and are incapable of assuring a world order with long-term stability under humanistic conditions. The strategy for the future outlined here is addressed to the peoples of the world. It is a strategy for the people, by the people. The individual, multiplied by three and soon four thousand millions, is the first hope and the mainstay of the human future.

Public officials and leadership figures would reject such a stance as hopelessly naïve. How can individuals have an effective impact on the running of the complex technological world, where power is concentrated in the hands of small elites as it has seldom been before? The position that individuals are the key to world-order reform can be defended, however, by answering two kinds of queries with respect to them. First, that individuals *can* indeed do something effective in the area of world order. Second, that they *ought* to do something about this problem. If individual persons, when acting in sufficient numbers and with sufficient motivation, both can do something about world order and believe that they ought to do whatever they can, our trust in them is warranted.

According to a famous philosophical principle, "ought implies can"; in other words, nobody can be expected to do something that is not realistically within his power of doing. But being able to do something is not in itself a good reason for doing it, nor indeed a sufficient motivation for it. Hence we must discuss both the "cans" and the "oughts" of world-order issues and the individual.

## The "Can" Problem

One of the great stumbling blocks of purposive action for a better future is summed up in the question, "What can *I* do about it—being but one person among almost four billion?" Unless he is someone of unusual influence, for example, the head of a government or of a prestigious social, economic, financial, or educational institution, there appears to be little any one person could do to motivate purposive change toward a new world order. Even persons of unusual influence have to contend with constraints, such as public and professional opinion, institutional prescriptions, laws and regulations, and feel themselves helpless when confronted with questions of basic reform. But this problem is not addressed to them, but to the ordinary, average person, one of the almost four billion whose individual behavior seems not to make any impact on global matters. Can *he* do anything about them?

The answer is that he can indeed. Of course, one individual against all the rest is powerless. But individuals communicate with one another, and can jointly motivate all the changes that need to be brought about to implement viable strategies for the future.

What any one person can do can be summed up under three headings: (i) consensus formation, (ii) personal lifestyle choice, and (iii) political participation.

(i) *Consensus formation* is both a personal and a political step. It is a precondition of all further steps, big and small. A consensus on goals and objectives selects those candidates for public office who best express the values of their constituency. The behavior of such candidates, when elected to office, can realize many of the values underlying the consensus. For example, in the late 1960s a sufficient number of ecology-conscious representatives and senators were elected to office that a few years later the SST bill could be voted down, reversing a pattern of many decades. Even in countries without multiparty electoral systems, leaders are sensitive to the forming and reforming of consensus. (That a new dictator did not take Stalin's place was due to the broad consensus among the Soviet people on the negative effects of the "cult of personality." Present-day Soviet leadership reflects a new consensus: unlike Lenin and Stalin, Brezhnev and Kosygin are managers, not dictators.) Although it is true that a strong consensus can be suppressed for entire generations under closed autocratic regimes, such regimes thrive only in isolation—they cannot support the growth of contrary consensus in allies on whom they are dependent. To the extent that all polities in the world are growing increasingly interdependent, the growth of a world consensus on issues affecting humanity places progressive pressures on governments whose policies go counter to it. World public opinion emerges as a major force in world politics and therewith in the shaping of the future world order. An international public communication network reports on and magnifies new trends and forges links between similarly thinking people in all parts of the world.

What can consensus do for the future in concrete terms? It can do several things. First, it can bring about closer ties of solidarity between the world's peoples. This favors the emergence of national leaderships who no longer pursue nationalistic objectives in disregard for the consequences on other peoples. Supranational consensus can make for increasing intellectual and cultural exchange across national borders, and facilitate the sharing of group identities. The mobile segment of world youth has already gone a long way toward crystallizing a supranational consensus on values and goals; their children could start with more global values than their parents did and carry the process still further.

Consensus on domestic matters can be equally important. The rising awareness of ecological problems brought with it a noteworthy shift in institutional behavior, both in the corporate and in the political domain. Although more is claimed than done for the time being, the public's rising eco-consciousness has oriented many public and corporate actors toward conservation and environmental quality. A large corporation cannot remain competitive if news media continually report on its offenses against the environment, and few public officials can remain in office if they consistently disregard or vote against environmental issues. Consensus has similar roles to play in the areas of civil liberties, human rights, social justice, and equal opportunity in education and employment.

At this time the single most important objective of consensus formation is the demand for free access to full information on all issues affecting the human future, locally, nationally, and globally. Public officials and public media can sin against truth both by commission and omission. Partial reports and biased commentaries lend support to the emergence of harmful patterns of consensus, for example, by fueling latent parochialism, chauvinism, intolerance, racial and cultural prejudice, doomsday scares, lethargy-inducing pessimism, unreflective optimism, unconditional economic growthmanship, and so on. The individual can be expected to form a sound opinion only if he is well informed. The first duty of the public is to form a consensus with respect to demanding a free flow of relevant and responsible information.*

(ii) Then there is the matter of choosing one's *personal lifestyle*. The problems of mankind can be aggravated or eliminated by individuals depending on their choice of lifestyles. To be sure, an existence below the poverty line offers no choice of lifestyles, and has no role to play here. (It is one of the objectives of world-order reform to raise the existence of all populations above the poverty line, and therewith bring all people into the domain of personal choice and global self-determination.) But wherever living standards allow existence above the poverty line, they allow a choice among alternative lifestyles. As soon as we can choose to live in one place rather than another, or even to buy one product rather

---

* There are indications that such a demand is already shaping up. Maverick groups championing the causes of peace, social justice, the environment, stable population, and so forth, demand public access to information pertinent to their concerns. (See, for example, the proposal to create a "Global Information Cooperative" of War Control Planners, Inc., a nonprofit Washington organization dedicated to "a future without war.")

than another, we have a choice of lifestyles at our disposition, and with that a real option to implement particular strategies for the future.

It is often pointed out that a child born in the United States places a load on the environment that is forty times bigger than that of a child born in India. The figures hold true statistically, but they obscure the fact that there is no blind predetermination about the load any of us places on the environment. A high material standard of living creates a higher load than one below the poverty line, but how much higher this load is, is not written in the stars but in people's choices of personal lifestyles. The relatively affluent individual can still choose to drink water rather than an artificial concoction in a throwaway, nonbiodegradable container; and if he craves a certain kind of drink he now has the option to refill or recycle its container. Affluent people can still walk, ride buses or subways, and if they prefer the convenience of a private automobile they can choose between oversized and overpowered (and still unsafe) superwagons, and cars that offer as much room, comfort, and safety as the individual really needs, with a minimum cost in resources, space, and pollution. It is simply not true that it is "human nature" to always choose the biggest, the fastest, and the most powerful of everything. Already some professional and social groups have learned to make more rational choices, weighing not only the relative size of the price tags and their budgets, but also some of the broader costs and benefits.*

Beyond group-average, there are important exceptions on the personal level. Many a man in the United States, as well as in Europe, who drives a battered Volkswagen has a large

---

* The 1973/74 energy crisis helped to implant a new conservation ethic in many countries of the developed world. If its effects on people's thinking do not disappear with the lifting of the Arab oil embargoes, its long-term benefits may outweigh its short-term drawbacks: it may serve as an advance warning of a wide variety of system-generated resource limitations and of the need to cope with them.

record collection and library, or even a Picasso hanging on his walls. For each one of us, there is a real choice. There is no inborn drive which makes the 6 percent of the world's population that happens to live in the USA use 35 percent of the world's energy—and contribute 70 percent of its pollution. The person who enjoys winding his way through snowy hills can do so on skis or on snowmobiles; he can get pleasure out of biking and sailboating, as well as sitting astride four-cylinder monsters and holding the handle of a 100-HP outboard. The fun and games are not so different, but the loads on the environment are.

The impacts of such choices on world peace are also significant. As these lines are written, a commentator on a New York area television news program has advocated armed intervention in Libya and other Arab countries to assure America's oil supplies. He pointed out that oil is something we must absolutely have, and if it takes the landing of armed forces to get it, then that is what we must do.[1] If the great powers adopted such tactics as their standard policy, it would not be long before they would be confronting each other in fierce armed conflict over the globe's dwindling natural resources. Other voices caution that we could do with less oil—if Americans drove cars with an average weight of 2500 pounds rather than 3500 pounds, the nation would save one million barrels of oil a day; and a similar saving could be realized if the top speed on superhighways was dropped by an average of ten miles per hour. Driving lighter cars, and driving less fast, is a choice of lifestyle (driving styles are lifestyles, too), even if a small one. Personal choices of using resources and space and generating pollution only if and as needed, could make major differences. Instead of struggling—and perhaps fighting —to assure unnecessarily large import quotas, we could rationalize our consumption of nonrenewable resources, and do so through personal choices, rather than shortage-provoked crises or coercive legislation.

Personal lifestyles shape the economy, the social and political structure, as well as the environment. How each person conducts his life affects the globe and makes a difference to humanity's future. This impact goes beyond the direct consequences of one's own chosen lifestyle: it also affects other persons' decisions as it spreads to residential communities, professional groups, socioeconomic classes, and common-interest groups. Through discussion, and by way of personal example, trends in new lifestyles take shape. Each one of us can start a trend toward a healthier lifestyle through his or her personal choice and example.

(iii) Last but not least, there is *political participation*. The historical trend in most societies is toward progressive citizen participation in the management of public affairs. The limits and possibilities of participation vary with the political systems, but few systems suppress it altogether. Increased citizen participation in a society is desirable to the extent that the citizenry is informed of the true nature of the conditions and is permitted to reach rational conclusions. Political participation without adequate public information is just as dangerous as political repression; whether it is a leadership elite that forces arbitrary constraints on a society, or its citizens, makes little difference to the outcome. But political participation joined with adequate public information is the vital mechanism for transforming changing values and emerging insights into effective policies. Participation starts at the grass-roots level but need not be confined to it. A consensus reached at local levels can be carried to the successively higher levels of more inclusive social and political systems, and can have effective impact on the issues which call for international and supranational agreement and collaboration.

The strategy of popular involvement is premised on the assumption that world-order reform starts at home. It starts with the changing values, behavior, and demands of citizens, provides inputs into national political structures, and affects the external relations of states. Proportionately as provincialism is transformed into a more universal humanism, the external relations of states become internalized within emerging supranational structures. This development must be prompted from below, through the formation of new, stronger, and more adequate popular consensus.

Two sets of multiple-feedback causal processes are involved. First, the relation between popular consensus and national political development. Second, the relation between national political structure and international relations.

The relationship of national politics and popular consensus in the domestic arena may be understood in reference to the confluence of two flows: a "top-down" flow of policy decisions originating with the national government and directed at the citizens, and a complementary "bottom-up" flow of responses based on historically evolved but changeable values and attitudes proceeding from the citizens and impacting on the policy-makers. The importance for effective government of a confluence between the flows must be emphasized, because it has been widely held that citizens can be directly manipulated by their government. It has become clear, however, that the power of governments to sway public opinion and behavior has been grossly exaggerated. The majority of citizens do not automatically respond to speeches by national leaders but are guided by the values and traditions prevalent in their group or region. Recent surveys indicate that the public's political, religious, ethnic, and racial preferences cannot be significantly changed by the usual processes of government.[2] Least changeable are the masses of pragmatically administered capitalist societies, where the government fulfills a managerial function and is seen as the servant, rather than the master of the people. Here the average citizen believes himself the best judge of what is good for him, and tacitly equates his own good with the national good. Large but ideologically indoctrinated masses measure governmental policies against their ideologically colored perception of desirability; and combine their practical evaluations with whatever impact their ideological upbringing and continuing exposure produced on their values. Smaller nations with long historical traditions, like those in Europe, respond to policy statements in the light of the confluence of deeply embedded cultural traditions and pragmatic assessments of the needs of the times. Small nations that have recently gained statehood still find themselves in the welter of conflicting tribal and colonial values and ideals and may be more easily swayed by governmental decisions, especially if they originate with a charismatic national leader.

At least in the larger and older democracies, in whose hands much of the power to change the existing world order is concentrated, the long-term and basic determinant of national policy is the general thrust of domestic popular consensus. It is expressed in supports and demands, in voting patterns, in various forms of citizen participation, and, when stressed, in opposition movements advocating reform or revolution. It is paramount, therefore, to act directly upon the factors that influence popular consensus, with a view toward producing those inputs into national political structures which could result in a more adequate foreign policy posture. This brings us to the second set of mutual causal relations: those between political structure and international relations.

Without delving into a detailed examination of what determines foreign policies, we can outline general traits concerning the impact different types of political systems have on the formulations of external policies.[3]

The nature of the administrative structure and the leadership figures of national governments has determinate influence on foreign policy patterns. Administrations that are highly bureaucratized impose a great deal of institutional constraint on foreign policy decisions: bureaucratic mechanisms grow complex and develop a momentum and vested interest of their own. Executives must respect the morale of their staff and act more as arbiters of various policy recommendations than as free agents making their own decisions. They are surrounded by competing factions, each armed with panels of experts who have spent more time studying any given issue than the decision-makers can ever hope to devote to it. Consequently an executive's decision is often a function of satisfying various internal demands, attempting to avoid schisms and respond to public demands as well as to the situation itself. The latter is no longer the sole, nor even the major consideration in foreign policy matters.

In bureaucratized pragmatic structures, foreign policy decisions are constrained mainly by the established political structure, and are merely conditioned by the need to satisfy popular demand and the demands of external allies. In bureaucratized ideological regimes, the ideological component enters as an added factor. It need not enter as an overwhelming conviction but may represent established standards and practices, created by earlier periods of ideological fervor. In either case, it conditions the way in which the machinery operates, and tunes the problem-perception of administrative aides and decision-makers alike.

Young regimes in newly liberated former colonial lands, or in economically underdeveloped areas, have neither bureaucratic nor ideological constraints to contend with. They do have major problems, however, in establishing their nation's identity, discovering and evolving its culture, defending its unity and asserting its voice in the regulation of the affairs of its region. Since many such nations have neither long established traditions nor a national history to lend weight to policies and help orient them, their leaders tend to rely on charismatic leadership. Such leadership is dedicated to realizing future goals (which do not necessarily center on economic growth) on which the leaders stake their political careers. Their foreign policy decisions will thus be strongly influenced by what they perceive as a step toward realizing their visions;

often they are made mainly for their immediate domestic effect. Thus foreign policy postures are strongly dependent on individual leadership figures and their goal settings, in contrast to large and established nations, where a pragmatically or ideologically oriented bureaucracy removes much of the decision-making process from the accidents of leading personalities.

Popular consensus has an impact on all these types of governmental structures, though the impacts vary in intensity and manner of manifestation. Pragmatic bureaucratized administrative structures respond to popular consensus proportionately to the degree of deviance of the consensus from established policies and the violence with which the opposition is manifested. Decision-makers become aware of problems only when they emerge as a public issue, and strong voices of demand or dissent are required to elevate trends in public opinion to the required status. But when that happens, commissions and panels of experts are appointed to study the problem and report to executives. Much then depends on the way in which different boards and panels present their conclusions and press for their acceptance. In the short run, the executives attempt to handle the issues within the established frameworks of decision-making, using established techniques of analysis. These are designed to dissolve the problems rather than go to their roots. Instead of depth-analyses, teams of specialists take the issues apart and examine them in the light of their preconceptions. The executive himself reaches his decision conditioned mainly by the givens of the administrative structure and only in part by the demands of the situation.

But more sustained issues raised by public consensus have a different path of treatment. The failure of classical remedies prompts changes in advisory personnel and permits new voices to be heard. If their solutions are not accepted, or do not work, further changes are brought about, including the naming of high-level aides on the strength of public expressions of confidence. Fresh blood enters the stream of bureaucracy and generates new directions in policy-making. If public consensus persists at a high level on a given issue, it can lead to the downfall of the nonresponsive decision-makers themselves. The way is opened for a change in administrative personnel on all principal levels. To be sure, this process is relatively slow and calls for strong currents of changed popular opinion. But in an age of turmoil, where many issues crop up simultaneously and can gain public hearing immediately, rapid changes in popular consensus are not unusual. They have been associated with such issues as the environment, war, attitude toward opposing ideologies, national defense, corruption in government, and many more.

Established large administrations operating within the framework of a stated ideology—the prime example being a form of Marxism–Leninism—conserve other channels of sensitivity to changing currents of public opinion. They rely on widespread public collaboration for the fulfillment of announced plans, and make strenuous efforts to win popular feeling for their policies. State monopoly on the news media and advertising, as well as state control of the economy, the social structure, housing, and land development, make the "top-down" flow of signals from government to people a strong and often an overwhelming one. If nevertheless a nonmatching "bottom-up" flow develops on some issues, the administrative bureaucracy has the option of redoubling the propaganda effort, or modifying its policies. While it is difficult to estimate the choice in particular cases, the overall course of major policy changes in established ideological regimes (for example, in the U.S.S.R. since 1945 to the present) suggests that a growing public awareness of issues in the principal areas of social and political concern had a determinable influence on governmental decisions. The dictatorial regime of Stalin could hardly be maintained today, and even the one-man leadership of Krushchev could not be readily reinstated. The maturing of a revolutionary society entails changes in public values and behavior, and government has little option but to follow its main contours. This process occurs today in China, where the early fervor characteristic of ideological revolutions is giving way to more settled patterns of life, and brings about a more level-headed assessment of the international system.

Public inputs into nonideological young and revolutionary regimes are the most dramatically effective: they can make the difference between success and disaster for the leaders. Charismatic leadership figures rely on the effect of their projects and personalities to generate basic support (if not by the population at large, at least by the army), and shifts in public consensus are either matched by deft adaptations on their part, or bring about their downfall. This holds true whether or not the leader's vision is ideologically inspired or propounds a personal or a national dream. (Witness the different cases of Tschombé, Sukarno, Castro, and Allende, for instance.)

Although the time-frames differ, and so do the particular mechanisms, no national government is immune to changing popular consensus, and no change in national political structure fails to reflect changes in foreign policy. Hence if sustained and intense popular demand can be generated for giving due consideration to issues of supranational and long-term concern, the consequent governmental reorientations would have a direct effect on those forums of international cooperation where the issues must be treated.

The answer to What *can I* do for the future? is that each of us can participate in and promote the formation of consensus on issues pertinent to the collective human future; can choose and propagate personal lifestyles responsive to improving the conditions of global existence; and can take part in the existing frameworks of political decision-making as well as demand wider citizen participation on more and higher levels. The actions of individuals are the *sine qua non* of implementing strategies for the future. World-order reform starts at home: with the ideas and values we entertain, the objectives we pursue, the leaders we elect, and the way we talk with and influence those around us.

## The "Ought" Problem

Even if people can do much, and ultimately all that needs to be done to implement strategies for a humanistic future, it still needs to be established that they *should* do what they can. "After all, what did posterity ever do for me that I should do so much for posterity?" This question sums up the essence of the "ought" problem in relation to long-term world-order issues.

The straightforward answer to the question about posterity is negative. Posterity never did anything for anyone in his own lifetime, for the simple reason that posterity only begins when that lifetime is over—at least as far as the individual is concerned. If the simple fact that posterity never did anything for them would effectively stop people from doing anything for posterity we would not be here: our forefathers would long ago have squandered on themselves all resources they could muster, and would have neglected to set up those institutions, laws, and customs which make for continuity and stability in social existence. Yet it is a remarkable fact that people show a great deal of concern for conditions that go beyond their own lifetime. They manifest such concern both in planning for the welfare of their own children, and in planning for the continuity and development of the societies and cultures they represent. Philosophers from Plato to Hume and Mill have noted man's striving for immortality through his achievements, his humanism, and his willingness to make sacrifices for a future in which he himself could not possibly share. Almost all cultures admire acts of heroism in battle, even though it is evident that the heroes themselves could not possibly benefit by dying for their cause. Without the cohesive force of concern beyond the immediate span of one's lifetime, the fabric of society would be ripped apart. It is noteworthy that older people have an interest in the future no less than younger ones and, until the advent of extreme old age, increase rather than decrease their time horizons.

Presently, a longer-than-usual time horizon is required if humanity is to make the adjustment needed for its experiment with global existence. How long? Jørgen Randers and Donella Meadows of the Club of Rome suggest that it should be our "cardinal philosophy" that "no man or institution in our society may take any action which decreases the economic and social options of those who will live on the planet over the next one hundred years."[4] Is such an extended time period a reasonable moral principle of action—apart from the fact that only a new religion is likely to have the force of bringing it about? Ought we to make sacrifices or refrain from obtaining benefits today, for the sake of the people of the next century?

Our capacity to predict just what action taken today depresses or enhances the economic and social options of people living one hundred years hence is, despite the computer projections of Forrester, Meadows, *et al.*, practically negligible. We cannot foretell the technological developments over the next one hundred years, nor how the present data gaps will be filled in. But we can foretell with reasonable cogency the consequences of some of our actions on the living conditions of the next generation or two. Even if our forecasts are subject to revision, we can tell what the limits of the earth are, given our existing technologies, our population size, and the current trends. Even without a computer, we can appreciate that the earth is finite, our technological capabilities limited, and that our mismanagement of the environment and of the factors contributing to population growth cannot continue indefinitely. We can also tell that some contemporary trends lead to increased tensions and may conduce to violent warfare, in which all parties will be losers. *Ought* we then to have at least a moderate time horizon, and condemn actions which we *know* to have dangerous consequences as undesirable, and indeed, as unethical?

If it were merely a matter of making life somewhat more difficult for the next generation, many people would shrug off such an idea—after all, previous generations sometimes lived under rather inauspicious conditions of existence and managed to handle them; moreover there were always those who had a good life, even in difficult times. Besides, people are adaptable, and the next generations may well be happy under circumstances that today we would deplore. A simple drop in the average global standards of life is not sufficient to motivate a contemporary realignment of ethical and value perspectives. After all, what did posterity ever do for us . . . ?

However, the issue before us is of a different order of magnitude altogether. Depending on our choice of actions today, human life could be reduced to the level of bare subsistence within a generation or two. The earth could become a depleted, overcrowded, underfed, overpolluted, and violently competitive place; human life could become as it once was said to be, nasty, brutish, and short. Or there may not be any human life at all, or even animal and plant life for that matter. If increasing tensions erupted in nuclear warfare, radioactive fallouts could make the earth uninhabitable for eons to come.

These are not predictions, but outlines of real possibilities. We have within our power today to decide not merely the relative ease and comfort of future generations, but the future of human civilization, and perhaps of the entire ecosphere. Given these possibilities, as well as the option to stabilize the conditions of life on the planet while permitting growth to continue in all areas not limited by the relation of our technologies and population size to the finiteness of the earth, ought we to leave the choice to chance?

Because we are open systems dependent for our survival and propagation on the pertinent free energies and information in our environment, and because our environment is largely a social one (even our natural environment is now mediated by social conditions), both our genetic inheritance and our cultural heritage conspire to make us answer negatively. The values of individual, group, and species survival are partly genetically transmitted, partly encultured. No group can persist which does not inculcate in its members the value of its persistence, and condition the basic survival and reproduction-oriented motivations to respect the conditions of group coherence and endurance. Although individuals can opt out from any society, as they can opt out of life, their basic motivations remain survival and culture oriented.[5] The fact that sociocultural systems persist testifies to this. Hence no typical member of the human species, and of any human society within the species, can truthfully shrug off the question of biological and sociocultural persistence. He is a motivated being, strongly oriented toward seeking fulfillments which tie in with the conditions of individual, collective, and species survival and development.

As the level of interdependence increases in contemporary society, the chances of catastrophe accrue, and the question of survival becomes more acute. To deny its legitimacy is to opt out of the human condition, to a specious platform of value-free objectivity. It is to deny that one breathes because he needs air, or engages in argument because he wants to understand himself, society, or the world. To deny the objective basis of human valuations is to deny human needs, and therewith everything that is essential about man as a complex multilevel open system. It is not merely a theoretical fallacy; it is practical idiocy. For the value-free objective man is not only a myth—he is a monster. If he were real, mankind would die out amidst high-flown affirmations of the gap between facts and values, and the fallacy of naturalism (i.e., of confusing values with natural properties).*

The answer to Ought I to do what I can to bring about a better world order? is *Yes*—provided I am a physically and mentally healthy human being, an active member of my family, community, society, and the species optimistically called *homo sapiens*. I can commit suicide and continue ruining my health through unsound habits; I can also work toward conflict, war, ecodisasters, and economic crises. Nobody can deny that all these things are within my power to do. But at issue is the question whether I ought to do them. If I am normal, in the classical, full sense of the term as it is used to designate a nonpathological human being, I shall recognize that all my instincts, basic drives, as well as my fundamental encultured societal values, point me toward doing what I can to assure my individual survival and development, in concert with the persistence and evolution of my society and culture. There is a basic human nature underlying all the masks we wear and roles we play; it is the poignant drive to live and evolve, individually, communally, and globally.

---

* The scholarly arguments are given in several of the writer's publications. See especially *Introduction to Systems Philosophy*, Chapter 13 (New York: Harper Torchbooks, 1973), "Human Dignity and the Promise of Technology," *The Philosophy Forum*, Vol. 9, No. 3/4 (December 1971), and "A Systems Philosophy of Human Values," *Behavioral Science*, Vol. 18, No. 4 (July 1973).

# 4

# PHASE ONE: THE RAISING OF WORLD–SYSTEM CONSCIOUSNESS

The strategy of popular involvement outlined here is based on individuals becoming aware that they can do something about the future and that they ought indeed do what they can. This calls for raising their level of consciousness from involvement with parochial matters of short duration to global issues of the more long-term future.

The world order corresponding to a normative model of a functional and humanly satisfying world can be realized starting with the harnessing of individual motivations within the national actors of the world community. Impacts on national structures can shape foreign policies and prepare the way for the creation of a supranational functional actor introducing the required degree of control over the world community's vital processes. This is a long and complex path. Its analysis will be divided into three distinct phases, and several subsidiary steps within each. The early phases respect the constraints inherent in the present world order and set relatively modest objectives. The middle and later phases move increasingly toward the type of world order designated by our normative model, building on the momentum elicited in the preceding phases.

In a preliminary way, we may characterize each of the three phases of the strategy in terms of "eras." The first phase may be denoted the *era of world-system consciousness*; the second the *era of multilevel decision-making*; and the third the *era of global homeostasis*. The first-phase strategy seeks to loosen complacency and ingrained habits and values by raising issues that exhibit the inadequacy of present procedures to manage the future. The second phase is to realize a theoretical ideal in global practice: the initiation of an information flow and feedback process with multiple levels of responses, to achieve self-corrective measures without arbitrary and coercive techniques. The third phase seeks the real-world implementation of the theorized societal mechanism to manage the stability of a humanistic world system in the form of a universal functional organization with limited, but adequate, power and authority.*

## Objectives of the First Phase

The objective of the first phase is to raise the level of world-system consciousness through the widespread discussion of current issues and practices. World-system consciousness is to be raised to a level where it constitutes a sufficiently powerful input into national political processes to change the foreign policy posture of the governments with respect to the basic issues of global development.

Unfortunately, popular consensus still lags behind the needs of the times in most countries of the world. In the Third

* The three-phase strategy should be compared with the "prospectus for transition" given by Richard Falk in the *First Draft of the American World Order Models Project Manuscript* (1972). There the initial decade is devoted to the reorientation of national outlooks; the second decade to the growth of transnational developments; and the third to global structural developments. They are keynoted as the era of consciousness, the era of mobilization, and the era of transformation. The structural isomorphies with the present proposals are evident; a detailed reading will disclose, however, numerous differences (although few, if any, major disagreements).

World, people's values and objectives center on assuring the daily necessities of life, and beyond that on gathering personal wealth and influence. Collective values are mainly limited to discovering and asserting national, ethnic, and racial identities, and securing the nation a respected place in the world community. The popular consensus of Marxist–Leninist countries is permeated with various levels of ideological conviction which includes humanistic claims for all mankind and sympathy for fellow-Marxist countries. But the ideology also leads to dichotomizing the world's peoples into reactionary and progressive camps and tends to bog down in interbloc animosities and intrabloc rivalries.

The people of the Western world still subscribe, by and large, to the "invisible hand" doctrine inspired by the early phases of capitalism, which gives them the comforting assurance that whatever is in their own interest is also in the public interest. This doctrine is impotent to motivate any action where the individual must make sacrifices, however slight, in the interest of others, or even for his own more distant future. Immediate gain correlates with national good, and national good is also the good of mankind at large. Though not expressed in terms as basic as these, this attitude has been the mainspring of the great economic progress of Western-style capitalism. It was admirably suited to promote growth as long as resources were available for easy exploitation. But this same attitude entails tragic consequences when it encounters limits of expansion and the need to share scarce or expensive resources. Its nemesis is brilliantly described by Garrett Hardin as the "tragedy of the commons."[1] When the size and resources of the commons are limited, individual competition intensifies and, for a time, permits the enterprising actors to draw further profits. But eventually they exhaust the commons and bring about their own downfall.

Popular consensus in the contemporary world is still parochial and dominated by out-of-date modes of thought, inherited from earlier epochs. Rapid change in the conditions of existence has outdistanced our societies' abilities to adapt their aims and motivations. To rectify this situation, conscious and concerted effort is required to catalyze the worldwide emergence of "world-system consciousness." This is a consciousness of the interdependence of man and nature; of the unity within diversity of all mankind; of the common long-term fate of our societies; and of the dawn of global culture and civilization. Its image is the picture brought home by the Apollo astronauts, of a blue planet swirling in space, alone in its splendor in the vast reaches of solar space. Its consequence is the realization that individual values must be measured by their contribution to common interests and ultimately to world interests. That parochialism is a vestige of the past and a serious danger on the contemporary scene.

But how can one bring about such a consciousness in the many, often provincially educated—indeed, indoctrinated—peoples of the world? National governments still control many features of the propagation of values with respect to their domestic populations, and the governments of the great powers are the most powerful actors on the world scene. But their own consciousness is based on the perception of the world as constituted by sovereign nation-states having eternal interests but not eternal friends, and regulating their external affairs with regard to their own good. New inputs must be provided to world politics. These must transform public consensus into one favorable to the emergence of a stable and humanistic world order. Bypassing the traditional channels of top-down decision-making, our objective centers on reaching public opinion, mobilizing it, and transforming it into an effective instrument of global politics.

## Implementation of the Objectives

To implement the objective of raising the level of consciousness of people concerning the global scope of our problems and their solutions, we need both consciousness disseminators and potential consciousness achievers. The problem is to identify these groups within the fabric of contemporary societies, and devise the tactics whereby the disseminators could effectively communicate with the potential achievers.

This task calls for detailed sociological inquiry, specifically oriented toward particular societies and groups. Such inquiry cannot be undertaken here, and we shall content ourselves with indicating a general assessment in reference to the type of society most familiar to this writer as well as to the majority of his readers: advanced technological society, in North America and in Central and Western Europe. The assessment is likely to change with respect to other societies, especially those of the Third World and the Socialist bloc. However, the general pattern will remain analogous: we shall no doubt find groups of people who have already achieved some degree of world-system consciousness, and others who are likely achievers. In some cultures, especially in underdeveloped countries, world-systemically thinking people may comprise but a handful of individuals today, while in some advanced technological nations, especially those with small populations (such as Sweden, for instance), a significant portion of the population may already tend toward such a perspective. The pattern of distribution of people who come into consideration as potential disseminators of this kind of thinking is similar in most of the advanced societies of the West, and the following remarks are intended to grasp the similarities notwithstanding local variations.

(i)  *The Potential Disseminators*

Those who have already achieved a level of global thinking adequate to qualify them for consideration as potential disseminators are likely to have done so through a first-hand study of the relevant problems, rather than by relying on casual hearsay or occasional stories in the news media. Although the current level of interest in global issues—such as peace, the ecology, the exploitation of the oceans and space, and food production—fluctuates widely, and occasionally reaches unparalleled peaks (e.g., Earth Day 1972), the average level of concern and consciousness is still inadequate to assure that persons who are not already motivated and informed should move out of their habitual ways of thinking and espouse a global perspective. Hence the potential disseminators of world-system consciousness are likely to be found among those who are exposed to more than the usual pattern of information. They are to be found first and foremost among the civil servants actively engaged in grappling with transnational issues within humanistically oriented international organizations. The level of concern among international organizations, especially within the United Nations family, has mounted dramatically in recent years. In a sense it has culminated with the Stockholm Conference on the Human Environment, for thereafter budgetary cuts have reduced the impetus of planning generated earlier. But despite the financial straits of Maurice Strong's Environmental Program, there have come into being a number of ambitious agencies and programs facing the issues directly, and on the global level. There is UNESCO's "Man and Biosphere" program aimed at developing a scientific basis for the rational use and conservation of the biosphere's resources and the improvement of the global relationship between man and environment; the proposed Commission on the Future of the United Nations Institute for Training and Research; the work of the Intergovernmental Maritime Consultative Organization aimed at preventing the pollution of seas by oil; the programs of the Food and Agricultural Organization in soil conservation, water development and management, and conservation of marine wildlife and forest resources; the work of the World Health Organization in identifying, measuring, and evaluating air and water pollution levels; the similar efforts of the World Meteorological Organization with respect to air pollution; and dozens of smaller-scale programs designed to tackle problems of supranational scope. Those who work for such organizations are daily confronted with the needs of the situation, and perceive one or another aspect of the contemporary problems of unequal wealth, power, and distribution of biologic and technologic resources, of social injustice, and the environment. The personnel of these organizations are therefore excellent potential disseminators of world-system consciousness (and indeed the more influential among them disseminate it already).

Secondly, potential disseminators of world-system consciousness are likely to be found among those who have studied some aspect of the problems facing the world in a sustained and systematic manner. These are the "academics" —students, teachers, investigators—working in the area of the biological, ecological, and social sciences. (This is not to say, of course, that *all* persons in these areas have already achieved world-system consciousness, any more than to claim that *all* international civil servants have done so.) Thirdly, potential disseminators are likely to be found in the area of the physical sciences, where an awareness of the true nature and scope of the problems of energy, natural and technological resource, and pollution is rising. Fourthly, world-systemically thinking people are likely to be found in significant numbers among the intellectuals (in C. P. Snow's sense, in which they are on the other side of the two-culture gap from the scientists), such as writers, historians, philosophers, and socially conscious artists. Especially in Europe, these people as

a group have tended to move in the forefront of political reform movements, espousing radical ideas in their youth while
moving toward greater moderation in middle age.

The next group of potential world-system consciousness
disseminators is a small but important assembly of top-level
administrators and managers. Administrators of brain-trusts,
and also of funding agencies, research and development departments, educational institutions, mental health and social
service institutions and the like, tend to take in a wider range
of problems than the average citizen and, unless they are
strongly motivated to uphold the status quo, have shown
themselves open to humanistic and supranational thinking.
The top managers of multinational corporations have shown
especial concern with global-level issues of the long-term future. Their incipient world-system thinking may be due to the
personal acumen of those who made it to the top in international business and finance, but also to the fact that many
large multinational corporations actively seek a global, or at
least an anational, identity. Such identity is in the considered
corporate interest: it avoids the stigma of exploitation by foreign capital, of tainting by foreign ideas and practices, and
permits employment and marketing without eliciting waves of
antagonism. But even beyond concrete financial motivations,
some multinational corporations tend to foster a global point
of view and temper their operations with humanistic principles. For example, Honeywell expends considerable effort in
the interest of mobilizing public opinion for the prevention of
war crimes; Westinghouse takes a serious interest in public
information related to population and family-planning problems; and Gulf made a decisive stand on the South African
issue of *apartheid*. Moreover, large corporate entities fund
research and propaganda responisve to socioecological problems as well as to the peace/war syndrome, partly to improve
their corporate image and partly out of true idealism (witness
the efforts of the managers constituting the Club of Rome, the

funding practices of the Rockefeller, Ford, and Kettering foundations, and the global efforts of The World Institute).

Although top managers in multinational corporations form but a highly informal "club," their vision can contribute to deciding the success or failure of world-order strategies considerably beyond the extent suggested by their numbers. Their position within the organizations as well as in society lend their views unusual importance. The means at their disposal for disseminating world-system consciousness are also of exceptional potential.

We next come to people who are widely scattered among various professional groups: medicine and law, and the public media. Their existing organizations as such are not committed to world-order issues, but a number of outstanding figures in them have espoused humanistic causes in a global, long-term perspective. The importance of such people, especially those with high community standing and with a public image, is obvious.

We have therefore the following groups as potential disseminators of world-system consciousness in advanced Western societies, listed roughly in order of the probability that a significant proportion of their members have already achieved the necessary consciousness levels:

Civil servants working for humanistically oriented international organizations;
Students and faculty in the biologic, ecologic and social sciences;
Students and faculty in the physical sciences;
Students and faculty in the humanities;
Multinational corporate managers and administrators of educational, scientific, and cultural institutions;
Professional persons and people in the public media.

This classification represents an estimate at a statistical average with respect to level of already achieved world-system consciousness, and not a judgment of individual mentalities and potentials. Other groups may include people with exceptionally high levels of global perspective, but they are likely to occur with less frequency than in the above groups. The statistical character of this classification likewise does not preclude that some members of the listed groups could take entirely contrary positions, and profess parochial, chauvinistic, and narrowly ideological opinions.

Again limiting our inquiry to advanced Western societies, we can locate a number of groups that qualify as *potential achievers* of adequate world-system consciousness levels, given sufficient exposure. The most likely groups are those who have rejected the establishment values and the limited horizons associated with them. The first precondition of achieving a new orientation is to be free of the shackles of the old. For this reason (and despite a number of restrictions and qualifications) we may regard certain groups of the "counterculture" as good prospects for enlarged perspectives. The full range of the modern counterculture includes the more idealistic youth movements, the community-experiment groups, the drug culture, the drop-out faction of hippies and yippies, women's liberation, gay liberation, and the new utopianism. Negative elements with respect to global perspectives manifested by these groups are tendencies toward isolationism, rejection of the necessary together with the unnecessary aspects of contemporary life, the espousal of specific objectives to redress imagined or real grievances, and naïve goals and expectations. Positive elements include mainly the rejection of the status quo and the establishment structure dedicated to its preservation. There is often a fine line between a rejectionist ideology that is still open even if it has already hit upon some ideas or ideals as positive goals, and an evangelistic spirit dedicated to the single-minded pursuit of limited goals. The drug culture and gay liberation come clearly into the second category, and most members of the Consciousness III type of youth counterculture (insofar as they are not hooked on drugs) come in the first. Counterculture groups and individuals that are still open to new ideals are excellent prospects as world-system consciousness achievers; global thinking and universal goals could provide content for their aims and give flesh to the bare bones exposed by their struggle against some aspect of establishment society. That such consciousness is not antithetical to the group ideology of many counterculture movements is seen in their already exhibited leanings toward communal lifestyles, their rejection of material values and therewith the establishment "growth-ideology," and their despisal of the external symbols of wealth and conservatism. World-system consciousness parallels their transnationalism, especially in the youth cultures, and the meaninglessness they perceive in upholding narrow nationalistic goals independently of human content.

A second major group of likely world-system consciousness achievers is composed of all the factions that have some social or political axe to grind independently of, or contrary to, the policy objectives of a conservative government. These include progressive minority and ethnic groups, progressive factions in political parties, peace activists, champions of human rights nationally and internationally (e.g., Amnesty International), and the promoters of regionalization and of supranational alliances beyond the pale of existing governmental initiatives. These groups often have no specific world-order philosophy, but they too reject some aspect of the status quo and seek a "better world." Although they are dedicated to specific objectives, these tend to harmonize with world-system thinking. Few if any such groups are dedicated to the maximization of individual or national wealth independently of broader concerns, and they all perceive numerous areas in which the current system of national or international order is in need of reform. Cogent general concepts concerning stability and optimum-states in the world system are likely to find fertile ground in their midst.

Last in this list, but by no means least in importance, are the great populations of blue- and white-collar workers. Blue-collar workers have been traditionally open to ideas of social reform in many parts of the world. As exploited by Marxist–Leninist agitprop-agents, these ideas first center on national goals and later take in a broader internationalism keynoted by the slogan, "proletarians of the world, unite." In the West, such efforts have not been highly successful, even if some factions of the labor force could be mobilized for political issues mostly of a domestic or local scope. White-collar workers as a class are more heterogeneous, including at the extremes liberals and radicals, as well as arch-conservatives. Members of this group tend to be more accessible to new ideas, but they too exhibit a hard core of personal and social values that prove to be relatively impervious to influence.

The above groups by no means exhaust the main strata of Western populations, but they offer the most likely prospects for containing potential world-system consciousness achievers. The remaining classes, such as farmers, small businessmen, as well as the upper-class members of the conservative establishment, are not likely to harbor a significant number of good prospects, apart from individual exceptions.

Our list of prospective world-system consciousness achievers shapes up therefore something like this:

Some factions of the youth and counterculture, those, namely, with a pronounced supranational community orientation;
Social- and political-reform activists, inasmuch as their particular objectives are humanistic and not tied to material goals beyond the war on poverty;
The great populations of blue- and white-collar workers.

(ii)  *Dissemination and achievement tactics*

At present the potential disseminators of world-system consciousness represent a small, but growing and influential, group of people in the majority of Western technological societies. They are the people who have already achieved an adequate level of thinking on their own, and who now have the social and moral responsibility for broadcasting this way of thinking to the rest of society.

The tactics of dissemination concern the ways and means whereby those who have already achieved global perspectives can communicate it to those who are the best prospects for achieving it. Although personal spheres of influence are important, the most efficient practices of dissemination are those where the individual places his or her prestige as an expert behind words and deeds. This calls for using social roles as the vehicles of communication whenever such roles involve competence in the issues of world order. Some of the more obvious communication tactics based on social and professional roles are outlined below.

*Civil servants working for humanistically oriented international organizations.* International civil servants as a class are beyond the pale of national identity narrowly conceived. They often work in foreign territories, and are engaged in projects which may not directly harmonize with national policies either in their countries of origin or of work. Persons working for humanistically oriented international organizations are thus somewhat in the limbo of a still-to-be-born supranational political system and its functional subsystems. But proportionately to the gain of influence of the organizations they work for, their views and opinions achieve importance. The higher echelons already have the ear of public media in discussing their particular programs and assignments; these discussions could also be used for disseminating the world outlook associated with world-system consciousness. From the relatively closed circle of international civil servants on foreign soil, missiles of urgent warnings and hopeful recommendations could proceed to national publics. Such missiles are already launched by concerned top-level administrators (U Thant's many speeches preceding the Conference on the Human Environment in Stockholm are a good example), but are not yet produced systematically by all major civil servants, whenever an occasion presents itself. Informal codes of public conduct among members of international organizations should include the recognition of the moral obligation to communicate their own already achieved recognition of global problems and the necessity for global-level solutions. The partially encapsulated class of international civil servants could then become an effective agency in the dissemination of world-system consciousness. Such activities would involve the civil servants as citizens of the world and would not conflict with their professional obligations; indeed, their involvement would enhance the effectiveness of many of the programs they are engaged in realizing.

*Students and faculty in the biological, ecological, and social sciences.* The primary professional objective of this group is to increase the scope and penetration of the scientific knowledge that supports world-system thinking. Students can use their organizations on campuses to demand more and better courses dealing with the pertinent issues, with the required humanistic and supranational orientation; teachers can design and suggest such courses. Given both the demand for and the availability of such offerings, curricular changes can be initiated in most institutions of middle and higher education. Scientists actively working in these fields can engage in further research on the pertinent problems, and lecture on their areas of competence not only in the formal educational settings in classrooms, but in informal meetings with students and with the community. They can also participate in forums offered by press, radio, and TV.

*Students and faculty in the physical sciences.* Following World War II physical scientists enjoyed an unprecedented position as engineers of a powerful technological society and workers of miracles for war and peace. In the 1960s this image became somewhat tarnished, because of the slowing

97

pace of technological innovations prompted by discoveries in the physical sciences (especially in the high-energy field) and also the dangerous and unpleasant spin-offs of many recent discoveries (fallout, deteriorating environmental quality, impersonal bureaucracy, electronic surveillance and invasion of privacy, etc.). However, with the rising concern over energy and resource shortages, people in the physical sciences again move into public focus as experts who may possibly help our technological civilization meet its almost insatiable needs. Students, teachers, and investigators familiar with the true nature of the problems can attract the attention of people with potentially open minds and raise their levels of consciousness beyond the range of provincial and national short-term goals. Increasing opportunities for such tactics will present themselves in the coming years as physicists, physical chemists, geophysicists, geologists, and scientists from related fields are called upon to testify before committees, function as panels of experts and as consultants to big business and government, and are queried by the public media.

*Students and faculty in the humanities.* The opportunities of humanists to attract public attention are less than those of physical scientists, but they too can generate interest and attention with respect to world-systemic issues and processes. Historians can trace developments from the past and project them into the future, as the new breed of futurist-historians do.[2] Philosophers can venture beyond the ivory tower of their specialties and expose views on the roles of conceptual synthesis, the adequacy of world views, and the intellectual climate (or *Zeitgeist*) of our age to their students as well as their community.

The role of students and teachers of drama, and the literary arts in general, offers different possibilities. The imagination of every age has been captured by its dominant literary trends, and such trends have often had a profound effect on public behavior. This is especially true of periods of national crises, elicited by wars and revolutions. Socially and politically conscious fiction, drama, and poetry has played its role in every major societal upheaval, both before and after the fact. Literature has proved itself capable of mobilizing popular energies and of concentrating them on particular objectives. What such literature needed is good subject matter, with substantive human content. Subject matter of this kind is amply available in the contemporary crisis of world order and its multiple options for the future. Most of this material still awaits exploitation. It requires the *literati* to study the real issues and base their imaginative themes upon a foundation of reality rather than on pure fancy. If science fiction could catch on, with nothing very much more substantive to go on than some usually wild speculations on the technological spin-offs of natural science, how much more extensive and penetrative could be the literature of world-system consciousness, with its multiple possibilities of tragedy and conflict as well as hope and realization!

Artists and writers could indirectly foster world-system consciousness by engendering pride and ambition in human achievement. As long as people identify with a limited social or cultural group, they measure their accomplishments by contrast to those outside their circle. Competition and animosity may be triggered, leading to divisiveness and short-range, short-sighted goals. People's sense of belonging could, however, be raised to the level of mankind as a whole. Pride and ambition would then focus on collective human achievement; collaboration would displace competition as a dominant feature of intergroup and intercultural relations. World-system consciousness could be furthered by art and literature that celebrates the great examples of human achievement not for their individual or provincial significance, but for being human. Prose and poetry could portray man as an intelligent and trustworthy warden of the delicate orders of this earth, as a species striving toward the understanding rather than the exploitation of nature, toward beauty rather than immediate profit, and toward significance rather than shallow amusement. It might imaginatively contrast *homo sapiens*, worthy of its name, with other forms of intelligent life, alternative earth creatures or inhabitants of other planets. Such literature could instill pride in human accomplishment as nationalist literatures sought, and largely succeeded, in instilling pride in national achievement.

But with all this, we need not envisage the prostitution of art and literature for the sake of social goals. We ask merely for the humanism of artists, in giving consideration to the ultimate effects of their choice of topics. Art and literature needs the fabric of human life, of social and cultural destiny. It has a choice of portraying it in a manner that discourages the public and instills scepticism, or one that fires the flames of ambition for a better, more worthy human condition. In the latter respect it can choose between instilling regard for God and country, for white man or black, for Western culture or that of the Orient, or fostering regard for the pride in universal human achievement. The great works of history had elements of universal human truth and insight in them, from Greek drama, which, as Aristotle said, depicts the universal whereas history deals only with the particular, to modern drama, poetry, and fiction, typified among others by the works of Hermann Hesse (which, significantly, enjoy a revival among young readers).

If those who create, interpret, and promote artistic and literary works would themselves achieve world-system consciousness, they could be powerful disseminators of it without compromising their artistic integrity. They could produce a significant impact on current modes of thinking and behaving at all levels of society. There is room (and need) for a new Shakespeare of world-system-conscious drama, as well as for new comedians of this mentality. As the French and Russian revolutions produced a harvest of artistic and literary works addressed to all principal levels of society, and as every great social change had its own crop of transcendent as well as popular art, so the supranational but very human concerns of the present transformation of our social orders could inspire and inform the substance of artistic and literary production in the coming decades.

*Administrators, especially multinational corporate managers, but also the administrative personnel of educational, scientific, and cultural institutions.* Managers of large corporations have proven their ability to focus public opinion on selected issues in connection with the environmental and resource-shortage crisis as well as in such specifically world-order-oriented activities as sponsoring major research and publicizing its results (e.g., the Club of Rome efforts). Most large corporations devote some part of their public benefit funds to issues of global concern, but much more could be achieved if responsible corporate managers would promote tactics to raise world-system thinking consciously and in concert. The various facets of world-order problems often lend themselves to linking to particular products and activities of large corporations, and these linkages could be exploited in advertising and promotion, selling both the desired product or service and the relevant world-order issue.

As multinational corporations grow in size and power, they reach and surpass smaller national regimes and their influence on local politics accrues. Since their interests are not tied to national interests narrowly conceived but are supranational in scope, and since their long-term future is closely allied with the economic welfare of humanity at large, their administrators could profitably devote a large percentage of their available public relations funds to world-system consciousness-raising tactics. Although such consciousness may conflict with short-term interests, for example, in the sale of powerful, fuel-consuming and air polluting automobiles and power recreational equipment, the long-term interests of corporations must be premised on the availability of a healthy and large consumer population and must accord therefore with the humanism of world-order thought. The constraints of the evolving world system are objective, and whether or not particular groups like them or not, they exist and need to be taken into account. Farsighted managers do not fail to do so, and at the same time to exploit whatever potentials such time horizons offer to guide the production and service policies of their organizations.

Administrators of educational, scientific, and cultural organizations could foster world-system consciousness by encouraging relevant course offerings, research, and public information programs, as well as publications and conferences. The output of the scientific research and publication industry is increasing exponentially, but much of it is of strictly limited relevance, dealing with highly special problems or with local affairs and issues. A significant portion of this output can be devoted to world-order concerns without depressing the quality of the work. Here an important role is to be played by funding agencies. The pattern of resource allocations is already changing, as we noted in Part One, but a further shift would be desirable, explicitly to foster world-system research and information. New designs of curriculum, new adult education programs, civic and community information programs, and related activities, can include discussions of world-order issues, mobilizing and shifting public opinion from a provincial toward a more global orientation. Executives and administrators can use the decision-making power of their offices to this end, without compromising their integrity in fulfilling their mandated functions. The raising of world-system consciousness is in everybody's long-term interest, whether or not it harmonizes with short-term wants and shortsighted practices.

*Professional persons and people in the public media.* In the medical and legal professions a number of individuals have already given evidence of farsighted world-system thinking, but the professions as a whole have not dedicated themselves to fostering such issues. Hence a useful immediate tactic for world-systemically thinking professional persons would be to attempt to mobilize their colleagues through personal and professional contacts. Reputed medical and legal journals would respond to repeated demands for space devoted to larger concerns with the human future, professional meetings could include symposia on such topics, and individual doctors and lawyers might volunteer as panel members in public forums. The generally high standing of these professions in most communities would represent an important input into first-phase strategy, if their already farsighted and humanist members would take upon themselves to expand their sphere of influence among their colleagues.

Members of the public media have a greater per capita potential for realizing effective consciousness-disseminating tactics than members of any other group. Newscasts, documentaries, articles, as well as short and long films, can focus on world-order issues; and reporters, anchormen, editors, and directors with a good nose for issues of public concern can not only report on, but actually discover, events and practices of world-system relevance. At present, farsighted members of the media are individually dedicated to global issues, problems, and solutions, but the professions on the whole tend toward local and regional perspectives. Domestic issues dominate most of the United States news reports; North American and British issues occupy the central place in Canadian media; and the scope of European reporting is mainly regional, with the local bloc of a few nations at center stage (such blocs comprise the Scandinavian countries, the French- and the German-speaking nations, the Iberian peninsula, etc.). Similar restrictions on the range of coverage by public media can be observed in the Socialist bloc nations of Europe, in the USSR, and in Latin American, Asian, and African countries.

Although news is available practically instantaneously from almost any part of the world, much of the international news is filtered out from actual releases in favor of news of regional, national or regional interest. This situation could be rectified not by reporters focusing on news of mainly local interest originating in other parts of the globe, but by reporting and commenting on events of supranational significance, and exhibiting their relevance to local practices and decision-making.

The tactics outlined above can be oriented toward specific publics, as well as the public at large. If they are directed toward one of the groups that possesses particular sensitivities to world-order issues, their success may come sooner. Avant-garde art inspired by world-system consciousness may have an immediate and direct effect on many members of the youth counterculture, especially on those with a pronounced supranational community orientation. Course offerings and public discussions will impact on young social and political activists with nonnationalistic but humanistic objectives. Public relations and publicity campaigns linking world-order issues with particular products and services could induce value change among white- and blue-collar groups, which could lead to changed preferences, for example, for more energy-efficient cars, recyclable or biodegradable containers, longer product life-expectancies, and production and trade practices commensurate with global conditions.

## A Scenario for Transition

(i) *Steps*

Phase one is the initial and immediately effective phase of a three-phase strategy. Its overall objective is to permit the rapid unfolding of a sufficient level of consensus on world-order issues to permit the more concrete projects of phase two to be realized. The phase-one objective does not include convincing large populations of the cogency of particular world-order projects and specific policies. The task is more modestly and realistically limited to disseminating a high level of consciousness of world-order issues: convincing as much of the population in as many countries as possible that there *is* a serious world-order problem and that the "business as usual" attitude of selfish and parochial concerns is unable to resolve it. The requirement is for a perception of the need for considered but deep-seated change in the way national societies manage human and natural resources and decide the fate of succeeding generations. The new need perception must precipitate first and foremost a call for more, and more reliable, information. It must awaken people from their complacent slumbers and move them toward demands, if not immediately for wide-scale action, at least for sufficient reforms in organizational structure to render society sensitive to such issues and capable of responding to them. The task of the first phase is to call for the kind of information-flow and response mechanisms provided in the second. Phase two can then carry the ball and lead the way toward the more concrete supranational guidance system of phase three.

The structural detail of the phase-one scenario includes the following steps:

Step 1. *Intensifying interest in global problems of a humanistic nature in the ranks of the intellectual elites.* Student demands and faculty proposals result in new course offerings, mainly within the biological, ecological, social, and physical sciences, but also within philosophy, history, literature, and the fine arts. Conferences and symposia are organized in increasing numbers and are progressively better attended. Officials of humanistically oriented international organizations, as well as teachers and researchers with known competences, raise their voices in their communities and comment on current issues and public affairs. Present trends and practices are challenged and a crop of new issues emerges into the spotlight. New plays, sketches, dances, novels and short stories depict alternative developments in the world and the fates they entail, and foster pride in human achievement as such. Poets give readings of works on analogous topics. Documentaries and promotional films multiply on television; public relations campaigns disclose the stand of major corporations on the issues. Professional men raise pertinent questions concerning the methods and ethics of treating world-order related problems. An increasing percentage of the research output of major scientific and cultural institutions focuses on world-system concerns; new programs of research and development are announced. Commercial exploitation of the new focus of interest begins, in the form of buttons, novelties, wearing apparel, entertainments, etc. It becomes fashionable to espouse one or another viewpoint; comedians, actors, and public figures make increasing reference to the latest foci of discussion.

Step 2. *Increasing exploitation by the public information media of the shift in public interest.* The more serious and farsighted members of the media begin consciously to foster and channel the treatment of world issues; regular columns make their appearance, weekly television entertainment shows feature them, and they occupy much of the daily talk shows. Congressmen and representatives are increasingly asked to take a public stand on them. News broadcasts feature various governmental responses and report on the public reaction. International multilanguage publications devoted to raising and discussing supranational problems and solutions make their appearance and become popular with segments of the population that pride themselves on keeping up with the times. At the same time, intergovernmental conferences are scheduled on a regular basis, following the pattern of the

Stockholm Conference on the Human Environment. The United Nations emerges as the key administrator of work designed to face global challenges through international cooperation. Conferences on natural-resource conservation, safeguarding the environment, budgeting energy sources, global security through disarmament and arms-limitation treaties, population policies, and human rights receive extensive coverage in the public media and are the subject of intense discussion.

Step 3. *The emergence into prominence of progressive figures, from the ranks of the progressive branches of political parties as well as from some formerly countercultural and opposition groups.* Emerging consensus on the need for supranational cooperation and longer time horizons creates waves of popularity for new spokesmen, some of whom ride them into positions of influence. More responsibility is entrusted to humanistically oriented international organizations and more funds are channeled to them. On the level of national governments, new blood enters in different ways and produces various impacts. In the Western-style pragmatic administrative structures, the thinking of experts and advisers undergoes progressive change. New perspectives are used to evaluate issues and new conclusions emerge. As the special role of the executive is often to choose between proposals generated administratively, the influence of experts on aides, and of aides on decision-makers, results in new domestic and foreign policy postures. Domestically, there is greater willingness to grant license to broader citizen-participation processes, and to produce relevant and full information to citizen-groups on the issues of concern. Internationally, governments show less fear of delegating responsibilities and decision-making powers to regional or universal actors.

In Marxist–Leninist regimes with large and established bureaucracies, a similar process evolves with *sui generis* features. Leadership figures emerge from party ranks, moved to positions of eminence by changing patterns of need perceptions among workers and intellectuals. The cogency of party doctrines and policies becomes tied in with the new perspectives, as the basic tenets are suitably perused and interpreted. Concrete policies thus proceed under the joint auspices of ideological propriety and popular approval. The increasingly pragmatic top leadership adapts its stance to the new currents and assumes the best posture permitted by its convictions and objectives. Changes of personnel in high echelons may occur, as some top executives fail to gauge the trends or refuse to move with them.

The charismatic leaders of young, recently liberated or revolutionary regimes either adapt to the new patterns of political preferences in their lands or rapidly lose the support they depend on. In some countries leaders manage to adapt and become spokesmen for the new trends. In others they manage to contain them by incorporating some new elements into their programs. In still others, leaders bent single-mindedly on pursuing outdated objectives find themselves deprived of support or challenged by new leaders capitalizing on the growing disenchantment. Whereas large administrative structures incorporate the inputs gradually, in small doses, small and charismatic regimes may fall and be replaced by leaders whose charisma is more responsive to the changing patterns of consensus.

The new orientations may disagree among themselves on most of the issues confronting mankind, but agree on the need for closer international collaboration and the imperative of delegating more responsibility to supranational decision-making organs. A plurality of views are championed and a hundred flowers bloom. But there is more institutionalization of concern for universal human conditions in the longer time perspective, both on domestic and on international levels. And there is a growing realization that a freer flow of reliable information is the *sine qua non* of the making of responsible societal policy.

(ii)  *Time*

It is difficult to estimate the exact time required for the three steps of the first phase due to a multitude of unforeseeable factors in the international as well as in the various domestic arenas. Nevertheless, for the entire phase, one decade appears to be a reasonable estimate. Four or five years of step 1 seem to be sufficient to entrain step 2, provided it develops as outlined. In the final years of the decade the events described in step 3 could come about.

In the time span of the full decade of phase one, students who in the early years of it were exposed to world-order issues in their college education are ready to assume responsible positions in society, including practical politics. Elder conservative politicians reach the age of retirement and are replaced by younger men, who are generally more open to new ideas and more responsive to shifting trends of consensus. On the international scene, ecological problems become more acute as resource shortages multiply, energy crises spread, more and more lakes and rivers are polluted and oceans endangered. International cooperation among the major blocs in the areas of space technology, communication, trade, production methods, and travel reaches new heights, and the free flow of ideas and people over national and bloc boundaries increases. Tensions are not likely to decrease, however, as the gap between the have and the have-not nations continues to widen, and competition for increasingly scarce resources becomes more ruthless.

In a decade the problems will deepen and multiply; communication will be facilitated; and new blood will enter the stream of decision-making. If catalyzed by a conscious and concentrated attempt to inject world-system thinking into the conduct of national and world affairs, the end of the ten-year, phase-one period will witness a widespread demand for international cooperation; for accurate and unrestricted information; and for creating a citizen-participation system to permit concerned persons and interest groups to take an active role in the determination of public policy. Therewith the stage will be set for phase two.

5

# 5

# PHASE TWO: THE ECOFEEDBACK INFORMATION–DECISION FLOW

Conceived in general categories, phase one is the strategy of consciousness-mobilizing; phase two, of the organization of multilevel decisions; and phase three, of supranational guidance implementation. Since the latter phases are premised on the success of the preceding ones, it becomes progressively more difficult to forecast the concrete circumstances under which their strategies can be realized. Instead, we must rely on theoretical guidelines for outlining what is desirable and, given the successful termination of the foregoing phases, likely to be possible. As we move from phase one to two and three, we move into the more distant future as well as into the realm of theory. The function of strategies outlined now for the latter phases is to guide the imagination, prompt more detailed and accurate assessments, and provide a wide enough target to be achieved from a multiplicity of eventual initial conditions.

Phase two, unlike phase one, involves concrete action rather than predominant reflection and discussion. It moves the focus of decision-making from exclusive centering in the hands of national government to a broader basis which exceeds the nation-state in both directions, the grass-roots as well as the international. It is premised on the assumption that when people's awareness is raised and their motivations har-

1

nessed, their private and public behavior produces modifications in domestic political structures which in turn have repercussions in the supranational sphere.

Phase-two strategy presumes the effects of the first phase, noted at the conclusion of the last chapter. These include governmental postures more favorable to providing free flows of reliable information to citizen groups, and to establishing supranational forums for the resolution of large-scale, long-term issues. Given such modifications of state governmental attitudes in many parts of the world, including most or all the major powers, the prospects for achieving the objectives of the second phase are realistic. The objectives of this strategy are, to (i) systematically foster the growth of world-system consciousness among the worlds' peoples by replacing the relatively uncontrolled consciousness-raising tactics of phase one with a constant and reliable flow of information on all principal world-order issues, and (ii) translate the popular consensus elicited by the information flow into an effective political participatory process through the development of the appropriate multilevel response mechanism.

## The Ecofeedback Concept

How do we approach the problem of systematically instilling in the world's peoples the basic values and purposes which humanity must have to overcome its mushrooming problems? If present values continue to guide the fate of the global community, they will prove to be as inadequate as the values of village tribesmen would be to steer the conduct of a modern state. The values of the large majority of the human population need to be shifted from parochial and national orientations to the global perspective. We have assumed that people's attention can be mobilized and their consciousness raised by purposefully injecting world-order issues into educational and public information practices. But will people's thinking be merely enlarged to take in a broader range of issues without changing their basic orientations, or will they face the issues freely and rationally, and make adequate responses? A simple consciousness-raising tactic cannot insure the latter. That people now discuss space travel, rather than horse-and-buggy or local automobile travel, does not mean that they change their views on travel or the values they attach to it. They merely take in a broader spatial and geographic region, doing so with perhaps the same prejudices they applied to the local regions. The widening of the focus of inquiry is not tantamount to a shift of its presuppositions. But it is just such a shift that is needed to successfully confront world-order problems.

Faced with the recalcitrance of basic human perceptions and tendencies, a number of experts have recently advocated techniques to "psychocivilize" society independently of people's consent or free will. In fact, the concept of free will is often regarded as but a myth. Value change is to take the form of a manipulation of behavior by means of operant conditioning (Skinner), electrocranial stimulation (Delgado), and psychochemical drugs (Clark). Skinner argues that only if such prescientific myths as free will, consciousness, and dignity are cast off does man have a chance to attain a peaceful, rational, and humane society.[1] Delgado urges the development of behavior modification techniques through the electrical stimulation of the brain; by such means dangerous impulses can be brought under control.[2] Kenneth Clark, in turn, sees in the recent discovery of a large number of mind-altering biochemical substances, with effects that range from mild tranquilization to hallucination and trance, the means to "stabilize and make dominant the moral and ethical propensities of man and subordinate, if not eliminate, his negative and primitive tendencies."[3]

The psychocivilization of society evokes shades of *Brave New World* and 1984. The electrical and drug-induced modification of human behavior presupposes a degree of subordination of individuals to authority that conflicts with every ideal of a democratic society. Behavior modification through operant conditioning likewise expresses contempt for individual freedom and self-determination, and pessimism concerning the ability of human beings and societies to voluntarily adapt to new circumstances. Moreover, changing the patterns of stimuli merely alters the behavioral strategies leading to consummatory acts and leaves the values underlying the goal-settings unchanged. Basic values can change only if persons come to the conclusion that holding them under specific circumstances is futile or unreasonable. Most individuals can be manipulatively discouraged from holding certain values through the behaviorist technique. But this technique is an uncertain and roundabout way of achieving the desired end. Persons may persist in upholding their values in the face of prolonged adversity (indeed, our culture encourages us to admire and imitate such behavior), and even when they change values, there is no certainty that their new values will be functionally adapted to the external circumstances.

The psychocivilization of society, whether through drugs, brain control, or behavior conditioning, disregards the fact that people can communicate with one another, and that the result of communication can be a change in their value and belief structures. We cannot communicate with rats, pigeons, and bulls in this way, and the best way to control their behavior may be operant conditioning, electrocranial stimulation, or drug-induced states. The thesis represented here is that systematic communication techniques provide a much more suited and humanly dignified method of producing adequate responses in people than any coercive technique bypassing the individual's will and self-determination. To achieve adaptive value change, however, not just any form of communication will do. The method of communication must be systematic: it must exhibit the problems in understandable detail, outline alternative approaches to its resolution, and offer real chances of implementing whatever decisions have been reached. It must then feed back information on the consequences of the decision in relation to the problem, and prompt new decisions, likewise available for implementation.

This is not to naïvely assume that the simple expedient of providing detailed information on current problems, on alternative solutions, and on the effect of whatever solution was opted for by the subjects in a concrete decision-making context, will automatically convert people to a set of more adequate goals and values. Information from public sources can also reinforce people's attitudes and beliefs by offering grounds for differential evaluations. Yet a constant and consistent exposure to balanced information will raise people's level of awareness and bring into the open tacit beliefs and suppressed opinions. The result may be the disclosure of contradictory beliefs and incompatible attitudes. These will tend to seek resolution. The hypothesis is that the attitudes and beliefs of individuals tend to be organized into internally consistent systems, with the recognition of inconsistencies motivating behavioral and attitudinal changes aimed at reconciling the thus surfaced inconsistencies. In the most discussed theory of this kind, the "cognitive dissonance" theory, the motivation for reconciliation is proportional to the magnitude of the inconsistency.[4]

A systematic use of the information feedback technique will tend to cause people's implicit belief and value systems to become explicit, and to expose internal inconsistencies which could then motivate efforts to iron out the conflicting elements. If people do possess a sense of concern for their fellow men and for future generations, beliefs and values which surface as inconsistent with the long-term welfare of their behavior systems on successively wider levels of societal organization will tend to disappear. The resulting shifts in motivation can be translated into concrete political action by providing opportunities to act on the new insights in an organized decision-making context. Hence, without demanding or enforcing compliance, the effect of the information feedback can be corrective, if not immediately, then after repeated exposures; and if not everywhere and in every case, at least with a sufficiently high probability to make the ensuing citizen participation process a potent force in shaping a humanistic future. This technique we shall refer to as "ecofeedback."

Ecofeedback is a societal self-corrective mechanism centered on the need for, and potentials of, value-change. The word itself is patterned on the concept of "biofeedback" (with which the process has structural-functional analogies) and combines the root "eco" derived from the Greek word *oikos* for house, with the cybernetic concept of feedback. The intended meaning of "eco" is a wide one: it stands not only for the meaning it has in *eco*nomics and *eco*logy, but also in sociology where the term "ecology" denotes the distribution of human groups with reference to material resources, including the consequent effects on existing social and cultural patterns. For any given society "eco" means the "house" which is to be maintained by a continuous, purposively normed flow of information constituting a regulative feedback loop.

## Ecofeedback and Biofeedback

The functions and potentials of societal ecofeedback can be understood through the dynamic metaphor of organic biofeedback. The latter is the feedback of information to an individual concerning certain selected states of his organism. The information is normed, i.e., it contains recommendations concerning the alteration of his existing patterns of organic states. Experimenters have found that individuals have a large, and hithero quite unsuspected, capacity to control their own states in accordance with the recommended norms. (For example, rate of heartbeat, blood-flow to diverse organs, muscular tension, electric activity of the brain and the correlated sensations, all prove to be amenable to control by ordinary individuals. Formerly such bodily self-control was the exclusive province of trained Yogis.) Biofeedback furnishes a dynamic metaphor for ecofeedback provided that individual human organisms and multihuman social systems are dynamically analogous in the relevant respects. In general, dynamic analogies are not in the realm of fantasy but prove to be a consequence of basic system invariances, such as those associated with open systems maintaining nonequilibrium steady states through the input and output of energies and information. General systems theory identifies a host of such basic systems properties and functions, all of which are independent of the physical constitution and particular origins of the systems. (See the review of the relevant hypotheses in the Appendix.) It is thanks to such isomorphies between dynamically analogous systems that knowledge obtained in regard to one system can be transferred to facilitate the investigation of another. And it is thanks to dynamic metaphors that computers can be programmed to simulate the behavior of other, more complex systems of interest.

Biofeedback is a dynamic metaphor of ecofeedback if, and only if, multihuman sociocultural systems are isomorphic in the relevant respects with individual human organisms. The important isomorphies can be stated in general systems terms. It is known, for example, that in complex systems endowed with ultrastability, integrated system dynamics precedes and complements stereotyped function-performance. For example, in a living organism, each component phase of organic functioning may be a rigorously predesigned chain reaction—e.g., a metabolic cycle, a linear sequence of hormonal developmental and metamorphic stages, or a neural chain response —but a sheer assembly of such linear chains could never yield a dependable performance in the whole organism: the slightest disturbance in the chain functions would upset the entire complex and the organism would end up in chaos. As Weiss points out, there must be coordinating interactions to slow the racers and to speed the laggards commensurately; and that presupposes integrated system dynamics.[5] In fact, the organic functions commonly referred to as "controls," "regulations," "compensations," and the like, come under suspicion of being instances of organismic system dynamics rather than mechanisms with predesigned and ready pathway channels. Under such dynamics the appropriate response channels form *ad hoc* as manifestations of an integrated response under some such overall rule as "most economical maintenance of an ordered equilibrium state" or "attainment of a state of minimum free energy."

In complex social systems similar dynamics can be noted, and their efficiency must not be underestimated. Corresponding to predesigned linear chain reactions in organisms, social systems have bureaucratic, economic, and political mechanisms with rigid pathways of information-processing and response. But if social systems would operate entirely through these mechanisms, they would be nonadaptive to changing circumstances, and would soon find themselves out-of-phase in the changing milieu. But history tells us that with some exceptions (e.g., the Aztecs), not entire social systems, only their "frozen" bureaucratic, economic, and political mechanisms suffer this fate. In place of the dysfunctional preformed mechanisms new ones are substituted, as many social systems manifest openness and adaptation *vis-à-vis* their environment. Such flexibility constitutes a basic ideal of democracy where, it is said, institutions arise in response to felt needs. The fallacy of totalitarian regimes is the disregard of adaptive system dynamics in their attempted imposition of a preconceived structure. Order in societies is achieved not by preprogramming, but by a dynamic give and take of plans, demands, and responses. Such a process can be steered (in the cybernetic sense of "steersmanship") through normed feedback, but it cannot be totally controlled. Had human societies been totally controllable, the regime of a strong man, or of an ideology, could have been perpetuated by designing all sectors of society to carry out the desired functions. On the other hand, had human societies been totally uncontrollable, new demands, plans, and values could not have interacted with the social structure to produce the process of social evolution. Evidently, societies are neither chaotic or random aggregates of individuals, nor rigidly programmable mechanisms. They are complex multiloop feedback systems, responsive to the evolution of new needs, changing values, and revised perceptions of social reality. Given such adaptiveness, social change will be proportional to (i) the "felt need" (i.e., the level of awareness of new needs, correlating with changing values and revised perceptions of reality), and (ii) the openness of social organization (i.e., the built-in capacity of the structure to change in response to inputs from all levels).

Sufficient dynamic analogy exists between biofeedback and ecofeedback to give plausibility to the latter's operations. If in a society the level of need awareness is raised, and if that society's organization is flexible enough to permit citizen responses to affect its organizing principles, adaptive change will tend to be triggered.


## Simulation of the Normative World

The information fed back to people concerning their earthly abode (or *oikos*) must show both actual and desirable trends and conditions. Its purpose is to motivate people to transform the actual world by reference to a normative world which functions as a realizable and humanistic ideal. The information feedback technique need not include specific recommendations concerning the practical decisions for moving toward a better world. It is sufficient if it discloses the problems (the differences between actual and desirable conditions in specific areas and in particular respects), and permits people to respond to them in the light of their own judgment. It must then return the information on the results of various responses for further evaluation. By producing a constant flow of actual and normative projections, the feedback technique represents a world-simulation game, with players in real decision-making situations, and incorporation of the effects of the decisions in the projections.

The technique for simulating actual conditions in the world over a period of a few years or decades exists already and is being continually refined. The original world model of Forrester is followed by the improved models of Meadows and collaborators; a regional world model with more precise dynamics is under development by Mesarovič and Pestel; and international organizations as well as private research groups evolve world models in various functional areas, such as the ecology (e.g., the atmosphere and the oceans), international relations, and the economy.* The simulation of an ideal world is less advanced, but currently planned research aims at its development. In this strategy we assume that actual and normative world-simulation models can be evolved by the mid-eighties, when this phase of the strategy is beginning to unfold.

The normative world is simulated by reference to the global resources which, if equitably distributed, provide the

___

* Especially significant are the energy world model of the International Institute of Applied Systems Analysis in Vienna, and the international economic model ("Project Link") of the Wharton School at the University of Pennsylvania.

necessary (though not the sufficient) conditions of the satisfaction of the hierarchy of human needs. These resources include food, water, and air, needed to satisfy physiological needs; energy sources and raw materials, required to operate essential production and service technologies; literacy levels for operating educational services satisfying cognitive (and hopefully also aesthetic) needs; and tolerable levels of disamenities induced by technological civilization. Based on these parametric conditions, social structures can be maintained or evolved to satisfy needs of belonging and esteem. Without such conditions, any form of social organization will prove to be frustrating of many if not all need categories.

The quantifiable basic parameters are at least the following:

— Total energy potentials, composed of existing energy resources (e.g., fossil fuels), and available rate of exploitation of renewable or inexhaustible energy sources.
— Total pollution coefficients relative to life-support systems, associated with agricultural, industrial, and related technologies.
— Total space availability, composed of habitable and nonhabitable, urban and rural, industrial, agricultural, and recreational lands as well as wilderness space.
— Total water availability, in view of geographical distribution of fresh water, and saltwater desalination technologies.
— Total food availability, including natural and synthetic terrestrial and oceanic foods (given the present state of food technology).
— Total literacy levels, including availability of educational services.
— Total transportation and communication capacity, for persons, goods, and services, including the transmission of information of public utility.
— Total realized industrial capacity for transforming raw materials into goods and instruments for services, together with realized potential for trained personnel (i.e., technological hardware and software).
— Total raw material reserves (given present rate of consumption).
— Total human population.

Many of these parameters cannot be uniquely defined, and several others have to be redefined with every important technological innovation. For example, the total energy potentials of the globe depend on the technological utilization of what is available, and that depends both on techniques for harnessing readily accessible energy (such as wind and solar power), and on extracting energies that are not easily accessible, or of which the extraction would produce harmful side effects (for example, hydro-energy through the building of dams, oil through off-shore drilling, coal through strip-mining, etc.). The amount of pollution likewise varies with the application of existing technological know-how and with the improvement of the emission-control technologies. What is habitable space is not determined by nature alone, but by man's capacity to inhabit natural regions by controlling the climate, the water supply, vegetation, and other vital variables. The adequacy of water supply depends on the size of the population using it, and on the technology that can make water available in water-deficient areas, for example, by deep drilling, tapping of natural water reserves, or the desalination (possibly through nuclear means) of ocean water. The adequacy of the available food likewise depends on population size, as well as on food technology. Food is what the human organism can convert to biochemical energy through its metabolism, and the amount of this depends on the preparation of the substances available in the environment, and not only on the availability of ready-made or easily prepared nutrients. Global industrial capacity, like pollution generation, depends both on the application of technological know-how and on the improvement of existing methods of production. Just what constitutes a raw material relevant to human life and society is determined by the state of technology and its realized potential in industry; potentially every substance within reach of man is a raw material. Finally, literacy levels and transportation and communication capacities depend on human will, and correlate with partly economic, partly cultural and moral factors. These are highly modifiable, and such parameters need to be often respecified.

The total human population is the only parameter that is uniquely definable, provided present data gaps can be filled in. But the fuzziness of the other factors, their changeability, and data gaps still existing with regard to them, do not mean that a simulation of actual and desirable trends could not be produced. These factors mean only that no single "run" is adequate to cover all reasonable possibilities, and that we must produce a statistical model incorporating probabilistic estimates of likely developments. Actual and normative world simulations can then be produced through the use of standard techniques in probability theory, computed with the help of sophisticated hardware.

The normative world simulation constitutes our probabilistic estimate of the necessary constellation of global resources for satisfying the hierarchy of human needs. The state of the world in which this constellation occurs is the *optimum-state*. This is not a state defined by absolute values, but represents the optimum combination of the available resources and technologies with regard to the existing populations over the time-span of a few generations. The normative world thus offers a general humanistic objective which is free of further ideological and moral content. It is transcultural in that the basic parameters it seeks to optimize are the necessary conditions of all levels of need fulfillments and are therewith resources for the unfolding of all cultures.

The developmental curves leading from present conditions toward an optimum-state function as the basic norms in the ecofeedback process. They represent the "preferred path" contrasted with extrapolations of real-world trends. Preferred and actual simulations may then be contrasted and evaluated with respect to current values, objectives, and the relevance of the processes to other aspects of human life.*

The ecofeedback technique is designed to let people respond to factual information relevant to their joint future and adapt their plans and goals to the realities of the global situation. However, such a technique is truly effective only if the participants appreciate the relevance of their decisions to the processes with which they deal. Hence it is necessary to construct a detailed substructure of the world, and locate any given participant within that structure. Because the world is a highly heterogeneous system, with multiple hierarchic levels and a large number of relevant variables, constructing a detailed global substructure is a colossal task. At present we do not have anything like an adequate model, but the pace of current research and development entitles one to hope that within the next decade or two breakthroughs may occur. Anticipating such positive development for the early 1990s, we can hypothesize some elements of the detailed world model, as it enters into the second-phase strategy.

The world model must be hierarchical, with levels ranging from any local system of action and decision, through intermediate levels, to the global level of the world system as a whole. Thus it must first observe a subdivision of the world into regional systems, and then a further subdivision into national, subnational, local, and neighborhood systems. The first subdivision yields seven major regional systems: North America, Latin America, Europe, North-Western Asia, South-Eastern Asia, Australia and Oceania, and Africa.† Each regional

---

* Such techniques are already used in contrasting actual and preferred curves for population growth, energy consumption, pollution levels, raw material usage rates, food supplies, urban growth, and so on.

† This division corresponds to standard practice, but there is no magic associated with this number seven. The Mesarovič–Pestel regional system model distinguishes ten economic subsystems, for example, although the tenfold division is dictated by mainly economic considerations and includes such oddities as "the rest of the developed market economies" including Australia, Israel, New Zealand, the South African Republic, and Tasmania.

system is further subdivided into national systems following existing political boundaries. Large and heterogeneous nations need to be further subdivided along geographic, economic, ecologic, or political lines into subnational systems. For example, the United States may be thought of as composed of subnational systems encompassing its states in the Northeast, South, Midwest, Southwest, the Rocky Mountain area, and the West Coast. Likewise the USSR, China, and other large and heterogeneous countries which show marked differences in their different regions. On the other hand, small and relatively uniform countries, such as Sweden, Norway, and Switzerland, may be thought of as constituting single systems. Others may conceivably be divided into a metropolitan and a provincial region (France, England, Austria, and so on). Subnational systems can be further divided into local systems. Local systems comprise urban areas following the boundaries of metropolitan regions, and rural areas following existing ecologic and economic interfaces. Finally, populated urban regions and extended rural regions are divided into neighborhood systems comprising a population of not more than two thousand voting-age citizens. (This is the upper bound for both face-to-face and electronically assembled town-hall meetings.*)

This process of subdivision is used to generate simulations of actual and desirable trends centered on the behavior of any given system of action. Thus people in neighborhoods can appreciate the impact of their immediate vicinity on their urban or rural systems, and the impact of those systems on the larger (subnational or national) systems where they are located.

The norm for any subsystem can be spelled out by constructing the preferred world model and relating the functional impact of the subsystems to its optimum-state—oriented

* See the MINERVA electronic town-hall system, below.

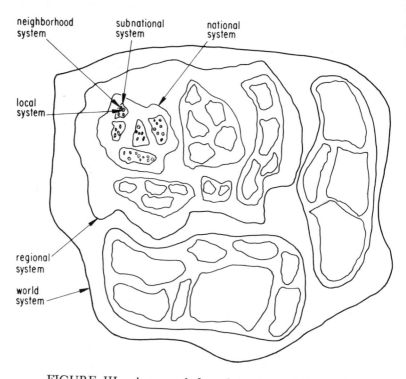

FIGURE III.   A map of the substructure of the world system centered on a given neighborhood system, e.g., a neighborhood of a few blocks on Manhattan's West Side. In the given case, neighborhood system = the designated blocks in Manhattan; local system = New York City; subnational system = New York–New England area; national system = United States; regional system = North America; and world system = the inhabited regions of the earth.

path of development. This involves the technique of "relevance tree analysis," based on the general principle that, in any hierarchical situation, the norm for parts-performance is system-performance. In this case, the proximal norm for neighborhood and local system performance is the subnational system's performance, and the distal norm is the optimum-state of the world system.

The "message" of the ecofeedback information flow is the

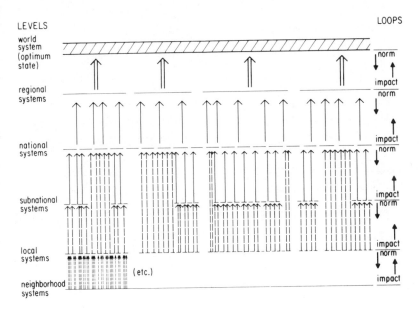

FIGURE IV.   Global Relevance Tree.

differential between actual and normative curves for any given subsystem. These differentials can be lifted out at any level, as illustrated in Figure V.

Normative projections for subsystems must be realistic: one cannot call for identical impacts on the world's carrying capacity by highly developed and underdeveloped subsystems. Equalization of impact could only result from a gradual process where each subsystem reduces its negative impacts and continues to exploit growth potentials in whatever areas are both compatible with the world's carrying capacity and are most urgently required to lift local standards of life above the poverty line. For example, highly industrialized subsystems must respect normal projections of reduced natural-resource usage and pollution-generation rates, whereas many economically underdeveloped subsystems face the need for reducing population growth instead.

The task of producing sequential normative projections for

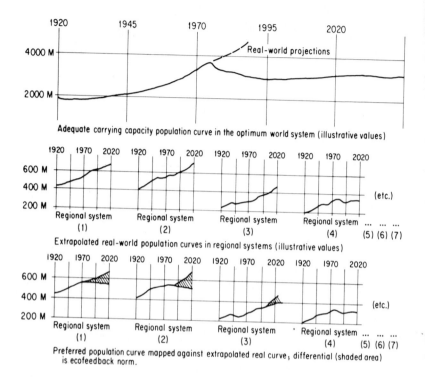

FIGURE V. The derivation of ecofeedback norms for regional systems (population parameters only).

systems on the various levels from the neighborhood to the multinational calls for large-scale interdisciplinary and intercultural research. But even if it enlists the best minds, it may commit errors in establishing norms for given systems. However, such errors do not have irreversible consequences: subsequent reviews of the effect of the projections on particular systems can reveal which projections had potency in motivating effective value-change, and which went wide of the mark. Periodic reviews of all projections are advisable also because of the rapid pace of technological innovations—these may affect the carrying capacity of the globe and hence call for a redefinition of the optimum-state of the normative world.

Successive reviews of the normative projections can correct for systematic errors as well as for changed conditions, and can zero in on differentials which emerge as especially relevant to the attainment and maintenance of optimum qualities of life for the full human population.

## The Response Mechanism

It is not enough to contrast actual with humanistically preferred conditions for all systems; the systems must be capable of institutionalizing the resulting patterns of value-change. In the absence of such response mechanisms the motivation elicited by the projections may be earthed in discussions, emotions, perhaps even in art and literature, but fail to trigger effective political action. The ecofeedback response mechanism must allow value-change to translate into decision-making, and to percolate the decision-making process upwards, from the critical mass of world youth and other motivated individuals to the top administrators.

There are two fundamental conditions for assuring citizen participation in the policy-making process: a widespread popular perception of a need for change; and an equally widespread awareness that the participation process is an effective means for bringing about such change. The ecofeedback information-flow is designed to exhibit to people the objective need for change in many areas of policy-making. And unless existing governments spontaneously carry out the people's wishes, the latter will recognize the need for instituting citizen-participatory decision-making as a precondition of achieving the objectives spurred by the ecofeedback information flow. Since some degree of governmental lag is more than likely, we shall suggest a possible structure for a multi-level citizen-participatory response apparatus.

The formal structure is that of the traditional town-hall meeting. Meetings are to occur at all system levels, from the neighborhood to the global. On the neighborhood level, the participants are individual citizens; on higher levels, they are representatives appointed by the members of the next-lower level. The meetings at each level observe the same general procedures.

1.  Information containing the following elements is presented: (i) definition of the area of concern (system behavior that is a potential stressor of the world's carrying capacity); (ii) extrapolated projection of the effects of the system's behavior in the relevant respect; (iii) normative projection specifying system behavior that eliminates or reduces its present load on the world's carrying capacity; (iv) simulated consequences of pursuing the real and the normative paths of development.
2.  Discussion is called for within established frameworks of parliamentary procedure. In the discussion individual members trade off their immediate interests against the value of reducing the exhibited differential. Objections to the cogency or credibility of the presented information are aired, and a consensus reached in regard to them. The discussion ends with the appointment of a committee to draft resolutions for handling the issues, to be submitted to the membership at a designated time.
3.  Draft resolutions are presented and the members polled in regard to them. Objections and recommendations for improvement are heard, and the committee may be requested to effect revisions. A time is set for presentation of the final resolution.
4.  The final resolution is presented and a vote taken. Representatives are chosen to bring the resolution to the next-higher-level town-hall meeting (if any).
5.  Members of the meeting report the resolution back to their own lower-level town-hall meeting (if any).

Neighborhood system meetings exclude (5) since they are composed directly of individual citizens. The global-system meeting excludes the provision in (4) to bring the resolution to the next-higher-level town-hall meeting, since there are no such meetings above its level. The meetings are spaced over several days or weeks, beginning with the presentation of the ecofeedback information and a period of reflection on it by the members. The first in the sequence of higher-level meetings begins after the last in the sequence of lower-level meetings is concluded. For each higher-level meeting, the interests of the members are defined by the resolutions of the next-lower-level meeting. On the neighborhood level, the interests are those of the individual members themselves.

When an entire "run" is concluded, a new run begins, with the issues arising partly from the resolutions at each higher level (which constrain the implementation of the resolutions at the lower levels), and partly from new simulations. The resolutions of the next run likewise percolate upwards from the neighborhood to the global levels, and redress grievances arising from the previous run, as well as treat the new issues introduced by the projections.

It is not to be expected that this process of sequential town-hall meetings can eliminate deviations from an optimum pathway of system development without residuals. Perfect deviation-reducing systems belong to the realm of axiomatics; real-world systems can only tend toward deviation-reduction through gradual processes of goal-seeking and information feedback. But the necessary self-regulative capacity for effective deviation-reduction over time is built directly into this strategy. The results of one run produce some changes in system behavior, and the changes are mapped and fed back to the system-levels in the next run (in the form of modifications of the extrapolated curves of real development). Normative projections are likewise revised in the light of new information relevant to the normative world model's specification of the optimum-state. Consequently the differentials between real and normal curves change from run to run, and reflect the latest needs for altering system behaviors. The new run of meetings can deal with updated information, and observe the effects of its own past resolutions. This offers the standard elements of purposive goal-seeking activity: clear definition of the target, and information feedback on the success of ongoing strategies for achieving it.

Ecofeedback coupled with a flexible response mechanism represents dynamic self-regulation in a multiechelon system. Systems of this kind are composed of echelons of subsystems which are themselves goal-setting decision units, coordinated at the next-higher level. The function of the higher unit is not one of control but of coordination. Goals are not defined inflexibly from the top and imposed on the lower levels; the goal-setting of the whole system results from the interaction of subsystem goals inasmuch as they can be coordinated in a pattern that maintains the entire system. All echelons enter as decision-making units within a network of coordination that enables the system as a whole to efficiently pursue an integrated set of objectives.

## A Scenario for Transition

(i)  *Steps*

Step 1. *Emerging levels of public consensus prompt national governments to jointly support a central information source relevant to supranational trends.* The fruit of the consciousness-raising strategy of phase one finds manifest expression in the mushrooming of activism among intellectuals and international civil servants, the proclamation of events such as the World Ecology Year, the World Development Decade, and the World Population Year, and in the proliferation of international multilanguage publications centered on global issues and solutions. Major multinational corporations form informal but nevertheless highly effective associations, and entrust committees with promoting specific issues relevant to the economy, ecology, security, and population-size of the world.

National governments find themselves confronted with organized actors, many of whom are highly powerful (already at the time of writing, of the one hundred wealthiest actors in the mixed class of nations and multinational corporations, over half are corporations), and face internal demands for adaptation to the realities of the global situation. Responding to these pressures, national leaders in one state after another agree to delegate certain functions and responsibilities to supranationally constituted bodies. The first result of the new foreign policy postures is the international agreement to create a common information source relevant to trends in world security, economy, ecology, and population growth.

The resources of many existing information-gathering and -disseminating national and international organizations are pooled, with nongovernmental organizations functioning in an advisory capacity. Existing hardware and software technologies are surveyed for adequacy and missing elements developed. A multimedia global information network is assembled, based on the use of existing networks and the addition of new components. It is established under the aegis of the United Nations and provided with access to information on the mandated functional areas by the world's nations. Administrators to head the organization are chosen, who in turn assemble teams of scientists to set up the information network, the information analysis teams, and the specialized organizations in local areas to receive and pass on the information. A distributed information network with clusters of readout points is established, with multiple lines accessible to local public media. The global informative agency operates as a super wire-service but uses the latest communications equipment, has direct and automatic access to essential data, and is restricted to the mandated functional areas (it does not interfere with the internal security and nonrelevant domestic affairs of nations). Its messages are converted into news items of local relevance, and are made accessible to all information consumers. Information is packaged for various levels of consumption, from the local up to the national and the regional. Appropriate media select the items and packages indicated for their level of operation.

The result is a constant and systematic flow of information reaching the world's literate peoples and keeping them updated on trends and practices which are relevant to their behaviors and critical for world order.

Step 2. *Rising public demand for citizen participation induces governments to agree to constitute town-hall meetings ranging from the grass-roots to the supranational levels.* The constant flow of information on global trends and problems mobilizes public interest and triggers the emergence of a host of public-interest organizations. These thrive under names as diverse as citizens' action groups, global-policy research centers, *pro bono* associations of lawyers, scientists, academics, medical men, and other professionals, corporate-concern committees, and social-concern national and international agencies. The momentum elicited by them is focused by public media specialized in monitoring, analyzing, and reporting their demands and activities and channeling their impact to legislators and government officials. Issues of intense concern emerge and take the spotlight of public discussion and debate. The need to do something more constructive than verbal activism becomes evident and centers on the demand for more effective means of citizen participation in all levels of decision-making. The available modes of political participation—voting, lobbying, participation in "private governments" in schools, hospitals, and other civic organizations, consumer and share-holder participation in the management of economic and corporate affairs—appear to be increasingly inadequate. Public-interest groups press for the creation of participatory governments on local, area, national, and supranational levels.

When public motivation reaches a critical threshold and is

focused by specialized and general-purpose media, legislators and government decision-makers agree to study and implement projects designed to establish a multilevel citizen participatory system where resolutions reached at lower levels are carried to successively higher levels and are traded off through discussion, representation of interests proper to each level, and new resolutions. Initially, the parliamentary processes of nation-states are switched into this sequence as its highest level. The national level commands executive and veto privileges not matched by other levels. However, further inputs from the domestic as well as the international arenas have a gradually moderating effect. Demands from the supranational sphere of regional and universal functional and general-purpose organizations and multinational corporations, complemented by the domestic sphere of citizen activism, combine to prompt national governments to surrender segments of their autonomy in making final decisions and carry instead the decision-making process to supranational levels. As information continues to be projected from the international top down, political participatory structures grow from the bottom up.

(ii)  *Time*

Elements of the processes described here have already been realized; others are still decades away. Pockets of ecological and social consciousness exist today that anticipate the eco-feedback information-decision flows and show that they are not unrealistic utopias but practical activities which require a sufficient level of motivation to become institutionalized. The current pockets of socio–eco-consciousness occur in medium-sized urban communities, mostly in towns with an important intellectual or academic community. In several such places (for example, in Düsseldorf, Germany; Vancouver, Canada; and Madison, Wisconsin) citizens band together to control their own future, using computer-generated simulations of the effects of alternative policies. Often, they are at pains to evolve norms as well as to test consequences. In some cases, they wish to involve much or all of the community. The "Goals for Madison" program, for example, has a broad community involvement as its objective, and uses a computer-based social, economic, and environmental model of the area to simulate and test various options and trade-offs in the realm of education, health, transportation, employment, housing, population, and the environment. The Vancouver program operates in conjunction with a computerized regional systems model developed by the University of British Columbia (the Inter-Institutional Policy Simulator) and is sponsored by the Board of the Greater Vancouver Regional District with the involvement of the other levels of government (city, regional, provincial, and federal). The model currently consists of eight subsystem-models: the human ecology, health care, population, capital service facilities, transportation, the economy, housing, and pollution. It is to be made available to all interested people, including policy-makers, policy-implementors, and private citizens, and is expected to aid in testing assumptions and focusing demands prior to implementation.

The noteworthy fact is that public consciousness in these places has been highly motivated to begin with. Students at the University of Wisconsin have been among the most outspoken and vocal in the country, and the people of Vancouver have consistently expressed grave concern with the future "livability" of their region.[6] Thus, at least on local levels, ecofeedback can be established if and when popular consensus achieves the required intensity.

For the ecofeedback flows on the full system level, the evolution of the operational instrumentalities constitutes an additional factor. When they are evolved, the final critical factor is the willingness of the political leadership to make systematic use of them. In order to propose a reasonable timetable for transition, these factors—the operational means and governmental attitudes—need to be briefly reviewed.

*Operational means.* This category includes software and hardware technologies, both for producing the information flow and for constituting the decision-making response mechanism.

The software technology for the information flow refers to quantitative system models of the substructure of the world, with probabilistic estimates of likely developments. Two sets of estimates are used to generate simulation models: estimates of what is likely to happen if present values and practices are not changed (even if technological development occurs), and estimates of realistic pathways toward global optima (likewise taking into account technological innovations). As previously noted, work on both types of world models is already in progress. Sufficiently sophisticated models may be expected to evolve in the next decade to permit computerization of the results for the world as a whole, as well as for any given subsystem. The print-outs will indicate differentials between the two estimates and thus point to the areas where present values and practices are in need of reform. The computer hardware for such print-outs already exists.

Gathering the data-base for the information flow is largely a matter of hardware technology. Much of it already exists, and missing elements can be expected to be filled in within a span of years, not decades. Earth-orbiting satellites already gather information on the following areas:

*Earth resources*—Satellites such as NASA's Earth Resources Technology Satellite (ERTS) observes and records the condition of soil, growing rates, rainfall, crop diseases and yields. Infrared detectors spot blight in crops before the farmer knows about it. If coupled with an information-analysis center, the ERTS system can tell whether a nation is headed toward crop failure or will have an abundant yield.

*Human settlements*—Satellites can photograph all settled regions and produce data for reconstructing human migration patterns, urban growth, rural development, and the colonization of virgin lands; and can assist in demographic surveys of the world population.

*Forestry*—Analogous scanning satellites feeding into data-analysis centers can keep track of the world's lumber resources and spot fires and other troubles more efficiently than ground observers, regardless of distance and location.

*Wildlife*—Satellites can plot migration patterns, track herds, and keep tab on ecological conditions affecting various species in all zones, regardless of surface accessibility.

*Mineral resources*—"Prospecting" satellites can discover mineral deposits, water, and other resources. They can also locate geologic faults and head off natural disasters related to the movement of the earth's crust.

*Weather*—Weather satellites already provide regular weather data on much of the earth's surface, and remaining areas can be readily covered by further instrumentation.

*Security*—Submarines cruising deep under the ocean's surface, tanks moving through dense forests, and military establishments producing or testing secret weapons in remote places, can all be surveyed through so-called "spy-satellites." Data analysis can complete information on any nation's military strength and strategic plans.

*Pollution*—Pollution effects in oceans, lakes, rivers, as well as on land, can be spotted, recorded, and their evolution monitored, through infrared cameras beaming images from specialized satellites. The ERTS experiment already produced important information in all these areas, and can potentially do so globally.

Transmitting the information evaluated at a data-analysis center to any and all habited regions of the earth presents no major difficulties. Echo-type satellites can pick up and rebeam signals from any location to any other. Both the information collecting and the transmitting functions of a worldwide eco-feedback information flow can be assured with present technology, with the addition of some further components which appear to pose no major difficulties of development.

Software technologies for the multilevel response mechanism are in a less advanced state of development, although here too, no basic difficulties crop up. Software technologies concern the legal codes and organizational structures providing the institutional framework for the sequences of hierarchic town-hall meetings described here. Citizen-participation institutions already exist in many countries and other forums are in process of development for accommodating decision-making groups on subnational and national levels. Growth must occur principally at the two extremes of the hierarchic sequences: the grass-roots level, and the supranational level. On the latter, existing regional and universal functional organizations could provide the necessary framework and precedent. A further growth in influence and competence of such regional organizations as the European Common Market, the Organization of American States, and the unfolding of organizations of federations of African and Asian states, can offer the forum for town-hall meetings on the regional system level, while a stronger and better functioning United Nations, including its General Assembly as well as its specialized agencies, can ready the setting for the global-level town-hall meetings.

The electronic hardware for conducting town-hall meetings on the various levels is in active development. In technologically highly developed areas, where traffic congestion, the rapid tempo of life and the sheer size of urban populations forbids face-to-face town-hall meetings, electronic intercommunication techniques become available that enable citizens to participate without leaving their own homes. The mass dialogue and response system developed under the name MINERVA (for "Multiple Input Network for Evaluating

Reactions, Votes, and Attitudes") is capable of handling small-group meetings of up to thirty persons through telephone conferencing, and small community meetings of up to 2,000 persons through the use of two-way cable TV.[7] Since membership size at all levels of meetings is relatively modest (the lowest level is restricted to 2,000 participants, and the membership of the higher levels is composed of the representatives of the lower-level systems rather than their entire membership), electronic techniques for meetings can be arranged wherever face-to-face meetings cannot. On the other hand, where the electronic hardware is not available, the technology-created pressures that obstruct face-to-face meetings are not likely to be present; hence the hardware can be rejected in favor of regular town-hall meetings.

Meetings on the higher levels can use either technique. If the problem is urgent, and the representatives constituting the membership of a high-level meeting are not physically assembled in the same place, electronic communication networks can be switched in. In other cases, face-to-face meetings can be arranged according to established procedures.

*Intergovernmental agreement.* The willingness of national governments to jointly support the information-flow and response mechanisms depends on the changes in the perceptions of the decision-makers, wrought by public demands from below and by pressures from multinational and international actors from above. Adaptive change is likely to occur first in nations where the regime is unstable and the domestic and international pressures pronounced. Stable regimes with large administrative bureaucracies will be the slowest to respond, especially if the administrative aides and consultants are conservative, or dominated by a doctrinaire ideology.

The process whereby pressure is brought on national governments is complex and includes a number of unpredictable elements. An exact timetable of transition cannot be proposed, but we may offer a general time-structure of development with probabilistic thresholds. Thus we expect that the agreement of governments to create a joint information-gathering and -disseminating agency will precede any agreement on the issue of creating a multilevel decision-making response mechanism. The information source is likely to be created within the constitutional framework of the United Nations, motivated by national pressures of public demands from below, and international pressures from regional, multinational, and global public and corporate actors from above.* Nevertheless, a period of five to ten years may well elapse, from the initial discussion in the U.N. of the need for a global information source, until its full realization.

The multilevel response mechanism cannot be established through U.N. channels alone since it also involves the domestic affairs of nation-states. Levels of awareness must first be reached within the domestic populations of states before sequences of town-hall meetings become desirable and feasible. Initial steps toward the institution of some citizen-participatory mechanism more extensive than existing varieties is likely to occur in relatively open societies within a year of the time that the global information network begins to operate; but fully constituted and supranationally joined policy-making processes in the world's principal nations are not likely to occur for another five or ten years—unless global conditions deteriorate dramatically and public motivation rises to correspondingly unforeseen heights.

Taking the publication date of this book as our reference point, phase one ends in the mid-eighties, and the global information-flow reaches critical mass sometime in the early 1990s. Phase two is expected to come to completion

---

* UNITAR's decision to create a Commission on the Future to produce annual "State of Man's Future" reports to the U.N. community may be regarded as a first step in this direction. (See UNITAR Information Note of May, 1973 for details.)

later in that decade with the creation, first domestically and then internationally, of the complementary multilevel decision flow. The creation of the supranational functional guidance system described in the next chapter would thus coincide with the beginning of the third millennium A.D.

# 6

## PHASE THREE: THE WORLD HOMEOSTAT SYSTEM

With phase three we move into the era of institutionalized global self-regulation. Although this is the last phase of the strategy outlined here, it is to be construed not as the end-product of sociocultural evolution, but as a transitory phase as well, leading to conditions beyond. It is a phase which presupposes the intensification of popular concern in the area of global issues; the recognition that global problems call for supranational solutions; and the prior implementation of a broad basis of decision-making, linking public-interest and citizen-concern groups with local, national, and regional decision-makers. Provided that world-system consciousness is mobilized, it leads to a multilevel mutual accommodation process; and provided that such process is guided by the inflow of full and reliable information, it leads to the emergence of consensus on the subject of protecting present and future generations from the evident dangers of out-of-phase development. The global functional guidance system is the concrete response to emerging need-perceptions, and the effective, though temporary solution to the common problems of all mankind.

## Design for a World Homeostat

Vast societal processes are not the products of human engineering, but can nevertheless be guided by engineered institutions. The world of phase three will not be a consciously planned world, but at best one that is consciously stabilized around states which offer the preconditions of human need-fulfillment for the world's peoples. Thus only the regulatory element of the world will be subject to social engineering, and only this element needs to be purposively designed. The warrant for such regulation is the danger of entrusting the evolution of functional trends in the areas of security, economy, ecology, and population growth to spontaneous processes in a world which is just changing from a heady period of practically unrestricted growth to one where planetary constraints suddenly limit growth and rechannel it to new areas. This is not to presume, however, that the values of a finite world with yet unplumbed possibilities and dimensions of growth could not become sufficiently encultured to render institutional stabilization superfluous. In that happy event, centralized global guidance can be removed to the shelves of history, next to empires and sovereign nation-states.

In the meanwhile it appears unreasonable to assume that a dependable form of mutual accommodation could evolve among the world's peoples without an intervening period of institutional guidance. Such guidance presupposes a design for a universal functional regulatory organization which, somewhat tongue in cheek, we call "the World Homeostat System."

The name derives from the functional isomorphy of self-regulation in warm-blooded organisms with the required self-regulation in the world system. In both cases a regulatory capacity stabilizes inherently unstable processes around steady-states which represent the "normal" or "preferred" conditions, conducing to well-being and development. In both cases alternative means may be switched in to reduce deviations from the steady-states, and the steady-states themselves are not stationary but quasi-stationary (stationary in some respects and not in others), and are, moreover, not time-invariant but time-dependent. Cannon himself (and since then a host of social scientists and biologists) noted the analogy between self-regulation in organisms and societies;[1] we may likewise draw on it in naming the phase-three universal regulator a World *Homeostat* System. But this name should not suggest that the system is either a natural or a permanent one. On the contrary, it is proposed as a temporary instrument of conscious social engineering, to ease mankind's transition into the age of limited material growth and pronounced social and environmental interdependence.

The problem before us is to describe and define the principles by which one can design a sociocultural policy-making and -executing mechanism capable of performing the tasks associated with global homeostasis. We shall proceed by reference to general theoretical postulates first, and provide operational specifications later.

The design principles of a global homeostat are the set of principles underlying the design of any control system whatsoever. These principles concern the coordination and control of functional processes in complex systems, independently of the nature of the components and the particular qualities of the system. Thus there is an isomorphy of control-system design when dealing with a house thermostat, the mechanism for keeping blood temperature constant, and with mechanisms for maintaining balance in an economy. Such isomorphy does not mean that the mechanisms themselves are interchangeable; it extends only to the basic functional relations among the components. It turns out that there is a set of relationships that is more effective than any other in controlling and coordinating certain processes in systems, and this set embodies the essence of the cybernetic control mechanism regardless of the form in which it appears. The design for a World Homeostat System is isomorphic, for example, with the design for a house heating system as regards the interrelations of the main functional components. This does not mean that the World Homeostat System is "the same" in any other respect as a heating system. The particular objectives for which the control system is designed, and the subtasks of its various elements, must be adapted to the load of each system: keeping a house comfortably warm in winter for the house heating system, and stabilizing the world around humanly advantageous functional states for the World Homeostat System.

In this design we first outline the basic structural features of the central guidance system (these features are isomorphic with other cybernetic control systems), and then provide it with specific content in view of its global regulatory objectives.

(i) *Structure*

The design we seek is that of a control system which regulates the states of another system in accordance with programmed norms. The two systems must be coupled by input and output channels of information and energy. The control system can, in principle, obtain the energies needed for its operation from *outside* the system it controls (as a heating system gets fuel and electricity from outside the house it heats). But control systems also exist which obtain the needed energies *from* within the system they control (for example, automatic pilots on planes and nervous systems in organisms). Obviously, the World Homeostat System must be able to draw all the energies, materials, and information it needs for its operation from the world system. If it does, the addition of the Homeostat System to the existing world system renders the latter *self*-regulative. It provides it with a mechanism to stabilize its steady states on levels where they offer optimum conditions for satisfying human needs.

Control systems require two types of inputs: an input of physical *energy* (which may be in the form of fuels or substances usable by the system), and an input of *information*, which the system can "read" and use to guide its active behavior. Such systems must have at least the following components:

*Sensors*, for receiving information on conditions in the environment which are relevant to system states;

*Correlator*, for storing and transforming information received from various sources;

*Receptors*, for receiving energy from the environment usable by the system in carrying out its operations;

*Accumulator*, for storing and transforming energy fed in through the receptors, and making it available to various system components for carrying out their functions; and

*Effectors*, for carrying out operations on the environment in accordance with signals and energies received from the system.

The components are ordered along two transmission lines:

Sensors $\longrightarrow$ Correlator $\longrightarrow$ Effectors (the information-flow line); and

Receptors $\longrightarrow$ Accumulator $\longrightarrow$ Effectors (the energy-flow line).

Purposive operational capability can be introduced into the system if we add another component:

*Regulator*, for controlling both the information and the energy flows in accordance with programmed norms. (This requires that the regulator have information of all inputs into the control system, and have access to the correlation of the inputs with the outputs.)

The *sine qua non* components and relationships can be assembled in an optimally simple design for a control system operating within a larger system. (See Figure VI.)

The same components will have to be respecified, and possibly subcomponents added, if the system is to perform specific tasks. This means endowing the basic structural framework with specific content.

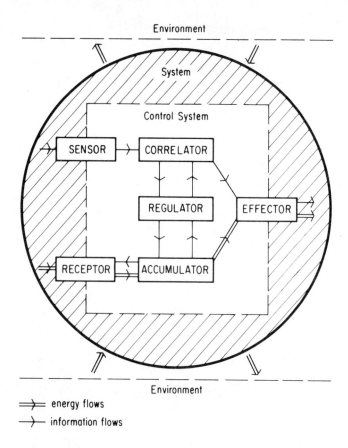

FIGURE VI. A generalized model of the basic control mechanism operating within a larger system (Compare with Figure IX in the Appendix).

(ii) *Content*

O. *Definitions*. The World Homeostat System (WHS) is a central guidance system operating within the world system and regulating its functional states. The world system is the totality of the social systems of the globe together with their technologies and ecologies. It is embedded in the wider environment of the ecosphere. The ecosphere is a region of structuration superimposed on the sun-to-space energy flow on the earth's surface.

O.1. *Objective.* The general objective of the World Homeostat System is to stabilize the world system around states which offer the optimum conditions of need-fulfillment for the entire human population. To assure this objective, the basic structural design in Figure VI is respecified to include additional components and provide specific subtasks for each. Figure VII gives the specific design for the World Homeostat System.

The remainder of this section is devoted to a description of the specific subtasks of the various components and their interconnections within the energy- and information-flow circuits.* These will be as brief as possible, since they are designed to stimulate further work in this area rather than give an exhaustive organizational blueprint. Besides exceeding the competence of this writer, exhaustive blueprints in the area of global guidance suffer from the "fallacy of premature specificity" (Falk); the current needs are to envisage the possibilities, rather than to put the finishing touches to complete but still utopian matrices.

ENERGY–FLOW CIRCUITS. Physical energy in the World Homeostat System is represented by the flow of funds, energies, and materials which enable its components to perform work. This basic circuit has the standard components of control systems, but the components are endowed with specific content, suited to the objectives of the system.

1. *The Receptor = The World Revenue Service.* The WHS must command a controlled flow of funds from the world system in order to assure the physical feasibility of its operations. Funds flow from three levels of the world system:

(i) From large national and multinational corporations that use global resources beyond the confines of a given nation; for example, in using satellites in space, mining or harvesting the

---

* Periodic reference to the design given in Figure VII will aid the reader in following the exposition.

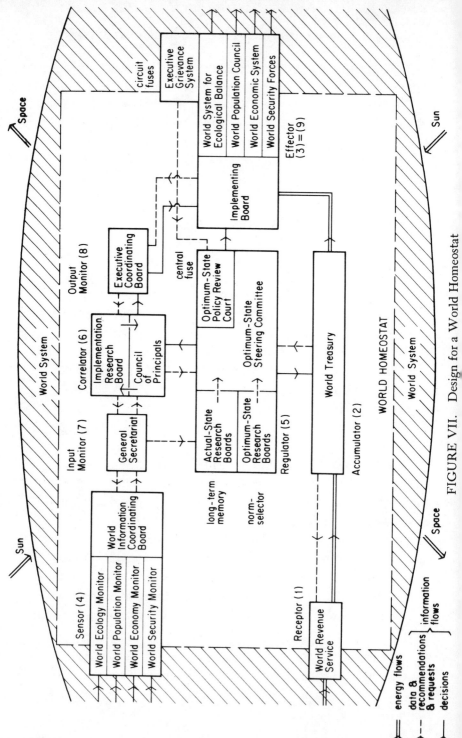

FIGURE VII. Design for a World Homeostat

oceans, dumping into waters that discharge pollutants into the seas, or polluting the atmosphere. Such corporations are taxed in accordance with their share of the global sources and sinks.

(ii) From national governments participating in the WHS, in accordance with their financial resources;

(iii) From private individuals whose level of personal income is in the superaffluent range.

The graduated progressive tax system provides funds for the WHS commensurately with the need for its services: actors that make the most use of the world system pay the highest taxes, and little or no burdens are placed on actors with modest means and rates of usage. Instructions for the collection of funds are prepared by the World Treasury, and implemented by the Revenue Service. If implementation encounters difficulties, one of the system's effector organs (The World Security Forces) may be called in to ensure compliance. Such action requires authorization by the central decision-making organs, on demand by the World Treasury.

2. *The Accumulator = The World Treasury*. In addition to the already mentioned functions, the World Treasury is responsible for resource allocations within the WHS. It submits to the decision-makers a periodic "WHS Operating Budget." The Treasury receives instructions from the decision-makers concerning any changes in resource allocations, and works out net budgets accordingly. Its task is analogous to the function of an accumulator in a physical control system: it is to receive, store, and transform the flows which enable the system to operate.

The principal energy-flow line connects the Treasury with the Revenue Service on the input side and the effector organs on the output side. The latter are the most costly of all WHS operations: they require relatively large-scale personnel, up-to-date equipment, and complex physical plants. The remaining funds go to the support of the administrative bureaucracies and their housing and communication needs.

3. *The Effector = The Implementing Board.** The energy- and information-flow circuits converge in the effector. The energy flow enables that component to perform work, and the information-flow directs its specific behavior. Since the behavior of the effector is its significant aspect, noting that it is funded by resources allocated by the World Treasury, we leave its description to the context of the information-flow circuit (#9 below).

INFORMATION–FLOW CIRCUITS. Information flows through the system and connects the various components according to definite functional patterns. Each component receives information, processes it according to the tasks assigned to it, and produces more information which in turn is received by one or several other components. Information passes among the components in the form of messages. These can be in oral, written, or electronically transmitted forms. Messages also pass among individuals and subgroups working within the same component: these are subsumed under the category of information-processing within the respective units.

We distinguish two kinds of messages: data-flows, and directives. Data-flows may have recommendations appended to them, but their effect on the receiver is not determinate. They are "for information" and not "for implementation" (although implementation may follow if the attached recommendations are accepted for action). Directives are for implementation, and carry the authority of the sender vis-à-vis the receiver. Not all receivers are fully determined by the

---

* I am indebted for some of the designations of the WHS components to Richard Falk's proposal for a Central Guidance System, in *First Draft of the American World Order Models Project Manuscript*, The Institute for World Order, January 1972 (in mimeographed form).

flow of directives; some have recourse to initiating review or grievance procedures. These represent data-flows in a direction opposite to that of the flow of directives. They may or may not result in revised directives.

The coordination of system operations can be described in terms of data- and directive-flows between components with specific functional mandates.

4. *The Sensor = World Information Services.* The WHS needs information on the world system relevant to its objectives; it can produce accurate functional outputs only if its decisions are based on full and precise data. To secure such data is the task of the World Information Services (the WHS "sensor").

The WIS relies on a global data-gathering satellite network for tracking and monitoring processes in the key areas of world ecology, security, population-growth, and the observable indicators of the economy. The hardware for such a network already exists, and has been reviewed in Chapter 5. The development of missing elements and the consolidation of the components into an integrated global information-gathering system by the year 2000 appears fully feasible.

Currently six different types of global information networks are distinguished: data-base, communication, computer, mass media, discipline-oriented, and mission-oriented networks.[2] A manifold of mixed-media technologies obscures, however, clear organizational divisions (e.g., tele-processing, satellite transmission, CATV, picturephones, videofiles, etc.). Experts foresee an evolution toward interdisciplinary information networks using a variety of technologies. (Some of these are indicated in Figure VIII.) It appears probable that by the year 2000 sufficient technological potential will have been realized to provide the World Information Services with a fast, automated, computer-based information-gathering, storing, and retrieving network. The software technology needed to operate a network that handles a large

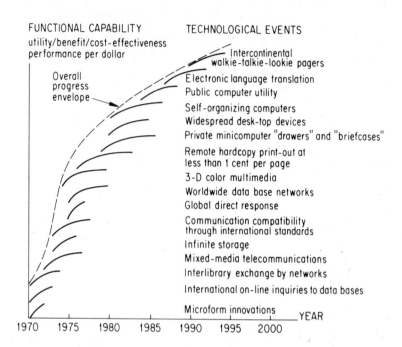

FIGURE VIII.   Estimated development of information-network technologies, 1970–2000. From K. Samuelson, "World-Wide Information Networks," *Conference on Interlibrary Communications and Information Networks*, Chicago, 1970.

variety of data with uniform symbolic languages is also under development and is likely to satisfy the needs in less than the time period forecast here.

The information-gathering activities of the WIS are designed to respond to the world organization's need for rapid and reliable information from any part of the globe in four functional areas: security, economy, population, and ecology. Each area is surveyed by a specialized monitor switched into the corresponding information network as a principal user. The four monitoring organizations are coordinated and administered by the Information Coordinating Board.

4.1 *The World Security Monitor.* The task of the WSM is

to detect violations of world security. This includes peace observation functions, reports on possible abuses of human rights, violations of disarmament agreements, and information on all activities that threaten to erupt in violent conflict. The organization is the investigative and surveillance arm of the WHS, reporting to the Central Information Coordinating Board, and undertaking special monitoring missions on request channeled through the Board. The WSM has no authority to procure corrective measures, although it can append recommendations to its reports, for processing by the decision-making organs of the WHS.

4.2 *The World Economy Monitor.* This agency investigates trends relevant to the mandate of the WHS in the area of global economy. Its primary function is to locate economic practices and tendencies which conflict with the goal of maintaining optimum capacity for human need-fulfillment on the global level. The WEM also keeps watch over the economic operations initiated by the WHS itself through its specialized economic effectors. Special requests for data are fed to the monitor through the Information Coordinating Board, and all data, with or without recommendations, flow from the monitor to that Board.

4.3 *The World Population Monitor.* The Population Monitor gathers data relevant to birth and death rates, centering its investigative activities on areas where preliminary surveys show a major discrepancy between normal population curves and actual rates of population growth. Investigations are initiated to locate the source of the discrepancy (which may be due to health conditions, unavailability of contraceptive devices, as well as to personal beliefs and values affecting family size). The monitor makes no decisions but reports conditions, with or without recommendations, for action by the decision-makers.

4.4 *The World Ecology Monitor.* Intelligence gathered by this agency concerns balance in the world ecosystems. It investigates practices and trends which stress ecological balance, and centers attention on areas where disasters or catastrophes appear imminent. The monitor attempts to identify potential bases of support for ecological reform movements, to enable the WHS to move toward ecological consensus by enlisting a broad base of voluntary support. Investigations of the agency include feedback monitoring the effects of interventions authorized by the WHS, and locating trouble spots suggested by the work of other monitors.

4. (1-4) *The World Information Coordinating Board.* The information gathered by the specialized agencies is fragmented, although the territory of which the information is obtained forms a multivariable but continuous system. The task of the Information Coordinating Board is to cancel any bias entering into the flow of information resulting from its segmentation by the specialized monitors.

The Board is an information collator and integrator. By subjecting the data flowing from the monitors to systematic scrutiny, it evaluates prevailing and countervailing trends, locates potential trouble spots, and follows up the implications of one set of data for another.

The concrete function of the Board is to periodically prepare a "Trends of the World Report" available to all decision-making organs of the system. In addition, it may be charged with preparing special reports on areas of particular concern, on request by either the Secretariat or the Executive Coordinating Board (cf. below). The operations of the Information Coordinating Board are successful if adequate and accurate information is available to the decision-making bodies to instruct the executive agencies to manage global resources and trends with minimum interference with personal lives and cultural heterogeneity. To fulfill its mandate, the Board operates a series of interdisciplinary research programs, manned by specialists on the lower levels and persons with increasingly wide ranges of competence on the upper levels. The outputs of these teams are transdisciplinary maps of high resolution on the lower levels, fed into lower-resolution, increasingly general maps at the higher ones. Information emerging with optimum clarity at each level is computer stored and made available for retrieval. Thus, Trends of the World Reports draw on the general maps, while special reports can delve as deeply into high-resolution maps as their purposes require.

The Board consists of the directors of the four specialized monitors and the directors of the interdisciplinary research teams. It is headed by an Information Secretary, who is the main liaison officer with the World Secretariat, in permanent contact with his higher-level counterpart, the Secretary General.

5. *The Regulator = The Optimum–State Steering Committee.* The Optimum–State Steering Committee (OSSC) is the central decision-making body of the WHS. It is not a government, however, although its constitution is analogous to that of national cabinets. The OSSC restricts itself to decisions concerning supranational issues which affect the availability of the resources necessary to meet human needs in the basic areas of physical survival, safety, group-membership, and esteem. Inasmuch as resources capable of satisfying such needs are available to a population, the OSSC encourages the development of conditions capable of meeting the higher needs of intellectual and aesthetic self-fulfillment. But the OSSC does not interfere with the social and political organizing principles of particular societies unless they thwart the basic needs of their members or prevent other societies from meeting their own quotas of need-fulfillment. Hence the OSSC is not an administrator and determiner of social structures, but a surveillant of trends with corrective capability. Its mandate is to optimize the globe's resources for satisfying the hierarchy of human needs for the entire population. It recognizes the functional equivalence in these respects of different political and social principles of organization, and the validity

of divergent ideals and ideologies of the good society and the good life.

The practical task of the OSSC is "optimum-state keeping." Similarly to peace-keeping, it is a regulative, not an organizing function. The OSSC informs political and corporate actors of actually or potentially antihumanistic effects of their behavior and recommends measures for rectification. If harmful behavior continues, the OSSC takes concrete steps to enforce corrective measures. These emergency regulative functions are entrusted to the executive organs of the WHS. The OSSC concerns itself only with the monitoring of trends, informing real or potential deviants of the problems, and issuing directives for corrective action if necessary.

The OSSC acts on the basis of two sets of maps submitted to it by its research boards. One set of maps informs the decision-makers of real-world trends and patterns. The other provides them with a continually updated optimum-state map. The OSSC acts to reduce the difference between the conditions indicated in the maps, with minimum interference with heterogeneity and development in all nonrelevant areas of concern.*

5.1 *The Research Boards.* Two sets of Research Boards are associated with the OSSC: the Actual–State Boards, and the Optimum–State Boards. The former is the system's long-term memory, and the latter its norm-selector (cf. Fig. VII).

5.1.1 *The Actual-State Boards* receive information on actual conditions and developments from the World Informa-

---

* Cyberneticians, systems theorists, and neurologists, as well as social scientists with a cybernetic–system theoretic bent, will have noticed several analogies between the functioning of the WHS and the CNR (central nervous system). Patterns of efference and afference match information inflows and outflows; decision and energizing centers function analogously. The likeness in function of the OSSC and of human consciousness is particularly striking: both are normative, pattern-matching, and operate entirely by information processed through other parts of the system. The latter analogy has been stressed in the political and organizational context by Deutsch (cf. "Toward a Cybernetic Model of Man and Society," in *Modern Systems Research for the Behavioral Scientist*, W. Buckley, ed., Chicago: Aldine, 1968).

tion Coordinating Board (the "Trends of the World Reports") and integrate the information with their own long-term memory banks to produce accurate "State of the World Maps." The Board consists of Special Panels manned by experts on processes in world economy, ecology, demography, and peace-keeping. They command their own specialized computer files and libraries. Data received by the panels from the World Information Services are placed within the context of the long-term history of the developments, and a map is produced which shows the dynamics of the processes over the relevant time-span. (This may range from months to millennia, depending on whether we are dealing with nuclear-arms conflict, with geological processes, or with a medium-range process such as agricultural technology.) Special maps of each type of process are integrated with one another as variables and vectors of the world system.

Producing an integrated general map of the world system is the task of a General Panel, composed of the Chairmen of the Special Panels and a group of "specialized generalists"—multidisciplinarians capable of handling information concerning all four functional areas simultaneously. The General Panel has its own computer files and library, specifically devoted to patterns of interrelation between the key variables and vectors represented in the special maps.

The General Panel submits its final product, the "Actual State of the World Map," to the OSSC.

5.1.2 *The Optimum-State Boards* define the global optimum-state by reference to concurrent data on resources, technologies, and patterns of distribution. The parametric values of the optimum-state provide the OSSC with the "reference signal" in evaluating maps of the actual state. The Optimum-State Board consists of Special Panels on each of the functional areas, and of a General Panel composed of the Chairmen of the Special Panels and multidisciplinarian consultants. Close collaboration between the Special Panels overcomes the dangers of suboptimization through the constant balancing of parametric optima within the context provided by the full set, i.e., the world system as a functional whole.

The output of the Optimum-State Boards is the "Optimum-State of the World Map." It is submitted to the OSSC jointly with the Actual-State maps.

5.2 *The Central Fuse = The Optimum-State Policy Review Court.* The OSPR Court is a central safety feature of the WHS; its task is to review grievances arising out of the decisions of the OSSC. Such grievances may arise within the Committee itself, through members who disagree with decisions reached by a sufficient majority to become effective (e.g., a four-fifths vote). If dissenting members are strongly opposed to the decision, they may take their case to the OSPR Court, where an independent assessment of the decision is undertaken. Grievances may also be channeled to the OSPR Court from Lower Courts, associated with the WHS executive organs. (See below.) If grievances arise which are due not to the manner in which the decisions are implemented, but to the sense of the decisions themselves, affected regional and national actors can file for review by the OSPR Court; the Court is accessible both to the decision-makers of the system and to those affected by the decisions.

The Court may vote to reaffirm the decision, overruling the grievances; it may vote to return the case to the OSSC for reconsideration in view of specific factors; or it may veto the decision and therewith oblige the OSSC to reconsider the entire issue. The Court's decisions are reached in the light of the consideration of the appropriateness of the decision for realizing the functional optimum-state mandate of the WHS. By providing a second forum for confronting the world situation with the needs for stable and humanistic conditions, the Court functions as a "central fuse," or additional safeguard system, at the WHS's top decision-making level.

6. *The Correlator = The Council of Principals.* The main

administrative body of the WHS is the Council of Principals. It specifies the decisions reached by the Optimum-State Steering Committee for effective administrative action. The Council acts as a control-system correlator: it matches the "empirical signal" provided by its own sources of information against the "reference signal" given by the OSSC. Its output is the "error-correcting signal" activating the specific behavior of the effectors.

The Council is composed of delegates from all principal WHS components: the World Treasury, the World Information Coordinating Board, the World Secretariat, the Executive Coordinating Board, and the Implementing Board. Its deliberations are based on "Feasibility Reports" prepared by its associated Implementation Research Boards. The Council may raise questions about matters of feasibility concerning OSSC decisions and feed back recommendations to that body in the light of its findings. In addition, the Council can request more, more specific, or different information concerning actual conditions from the Secretariat. Thus the Council occupies a central position in the WHS, having access to all its operations with the exception of grievance and review procedures, entrusted to the independently deliberating Courts.

6.1 *The Implementation Research Boards* carry out the research necessary to determine whether, and in what manner, OSSC directives can be implemented. OSSC decisions are based on the differences between the Optimum-State and the Actual-State of the World Maps, and are designed to reduce such differences. The Implementation Research Boards have the responsibility of discovering the real possibilities for doing so.

Implementation research is carried out by boards specialized to handle information pertinent to the specific level of the contemplated action. Thus if the OSSC decision involves pattern-modification in a subnational region, a board competent on that level examines the feasibility of implementation;

if the decision involves a multinational region, another board is consulted, and so on, for each of the principal levels (the local, the subnational, national, regional, and the global). The areas of research carried out by the level-specialized Boards include the following:*

*Local System-Level Boards:*
Energy sources and availability
Utilization of waste heat
Location of power plants: functions; transmission lines
Water supply
Conservation: management
Pollution: monitoring; management
Minerals: recovery; recycling; extraction; substitution
Land use: classification; management; restoration and reclamation
Heat balance
Housing and architecture: replacement; development; aesthetics
Transportation: public ways (roads, airports, rail lines, terminals)
Communication systems: utilization patterns
Information storage: libraries; microlibraries; retrieving; indexing
Crime control: public safety; court-procedures efficiency
Population: information; contraceptives; growth pressures
Medicine: health services; public hygiene; research; education
Education: school systems; curricular designs; distribution and delivery
Small-group relations: schools; civic associations; churches; professional groups
Group-living patterns: nuclear family; communal groups; experimental groups
Economic patterns: unemployment; inflation; incentive structure; income distribution
Organizations: management methods; decision-making; computerization; humanization

* This list draws in part on the urgent research studies proposed by R. A. Cellarius and John Platt in "Councils of Urgent Studies," *Science*, Vol. 177 (1972).

Public information: press; network outlets; private and underground media

Administration: management methods; use of technical
advice; party structures

Political subdivisions: number; size; autonomy; controls

Inflow-outflow: people; food; water; garbage and sewage; information

External relations: state, federal, regional systems; world
system

Additional research areas for higher-level boards:

*Subnational and National System-Level Boards:*

New energy source availability: breeder reactors; fusion power;
solar power; wind, thermal, tidal energy

Ecological limits on energy production

Water: nuclear desalination

Heat balance (system-level)

Weather control; effects of thermal pollution

Public ways (system-level)

Communication: information; crime control; population, etc.
(system-level)

New communication techniques: satellites; terminals of global
networks

Population balance: ethnic, geographic

Ocean resource use

Disaster-management capability

Migration and mobility patterns

Mass communications: networks; news syndicates; monopolies

Governmental policy: domestic; foreign

Social indicators; public-opinion polls

Crisis management

Mechanisms of stability and change

Constitutional design and redesign: checks and balances

. Defense and aggression potentials

Long-range planning capability

Legal system: laws; courts; penal system

Support of research: allocation patterns

Urban-rural relations

Realization of technological potential: urban, agricultural,
ocean, space

*Regional and Global System-Level Boards:*

    Energy, water, food, land-use, heat-balance, transportation, communication, population, etc. (system-level)

    Peace-keeping patterns and potentials

    Human rights preservation and violation patterns

    Arms control and disarmament

    Catastrophe management

    National and regional dedevelopment potentials

    Interregional population leveling: methods, economics, optimization

    National and regional value-differentials; cultural heterogeneity patterns

    Intergovernmental relations

    Support patterns of universal and regional organizations

    Nongovernmental international cooperation: corporate; cultural; personal

    International and interregional flow of ideas and people

The Implementation Research Boards obtain all information available from the World Information Services, classify it according to the possibilities they disclose of implementing particular kinds of directives, and complete the information where needed by drawing on resource persons as consultants. The boards obtain information from the WIS through the services of the General Secretariat (see below); and they prepare and file lists of available resource persons for special consultations when working on particular assignments.

The "Feasibility Reports" of the boards contain information on the transformation-potential of the local, subnational, national, regional, or global practice or trend which the OSSC seeks to modify in the interest of the global community. Each report contains a description of the pertinent practices and trends in actuality, and an assessment of their modifiability in the light of the existing knowledge of their parameters and dynamics. Jointly the two parts of the Feasibility Report enable the Council of Principals to specify OSSC-directed modes of action for the executive agencies or, if such action turns out not to be sufficiently feasible or desirable in the light of consequences or side-effects, to so inform the OSSC.

7. *The Input Monitor = The General Secretariat.* The Secretariat is the major go-between of the various components of the WHS, involved with the gathering and evaluating of information. It operates its own megacomputer, enabling it to respond to requests for information; to monitor existing flows of information for data gaps; and to store and make available all information passing through it. Secretariat personnel also satisfy requests for special assignments; for example, to constitute special-study research teams, send technical experts to provide assistance, and locate further experts for consultative roles. The Secretariat thus fulfills the traditional tasks its name suggests, operating under a Secretary General who maintains permanent liaison with the Information Coordinating Board, the OSSC, and is a member of the Council of Principals.

8. *The Output Monitor = The Executive Coordinating Board.* The Executive Coordinating Board is an oversight body for assuring that the directives handed down by the Council of Principals are carried out. It makes periodic progress reports to the Council, and summarizes problems as well as achievements associated with implementation. It can appeal to the Council for respecification of those directives that do not produce the intended results. Its recommendations may result in the respecification of the original directives and in revised operations. The Executive Board provides the final check on the directives passed for concrete implementation. Its Chairman assures liaison with the relevant organs by participating, *ex officio*, in the Council of Principals, as well as in the Implementation Board. The ECB computer records and files all information passing through the office and makes it available for retrieval by request from the decision-making, the administrative, and the judicial components of the system.

In this respect the Executive Board functions as the counterpart of the General Secretariat, but oriented toward the output, rather than the input, of the WHS.

9. *The Effector = World Executive Services.* The World Executive Services (WES) embraces a general Implementing Board and a hierarchy of specialized executive branches entrusted with concrete operational tasks. The WES as a whole is designed to combine balanced operation, responsive to multiple goals, with specialized efficiency. To this end it analyzes WHS directives and allocates responsibility for carrying out specific operations to its specialized branches. Its mode of operation is contrary to that of the World Information Services: it receives relatively integrated information, and dissects it into specific components. The two systems jointly enable the WHS to interact with the world system through specialized high-efficiency channels, without surrendering the capacity to process information in an adequately integrated manner.

9.1 *The Implementing Board.* The Implementing Board is the coordinating body of the World Executive Services. It receives directives through the Executive Board, and analyzes them with respect to the competence and ability of the WES specialized branches. The Board performs both a vertical coordination function, linking the Executive Services with the decision-making and administrative bodies, and a horizontal coordination task, surveying the performance of all executive branches simultaneously.

The Implementing Board matches funds received from the World Treasury with operations directed by the OSSC. This function is that of an effector; it is to use the energy-base provided by the system to carry out specific operations in accordance with signals from its regulator. (Cf. #3, above.)

9.2 *World Security Forces.* The special task of the World Security Forces is peace-keeping. The Forces are entrusted with missions by decision of the Implementing Board, in keeping with specific directives of the Council of Principals. The Forces operate as a police force rather than an army. Their primary objective is effective peace-keeping action without loss of life or permanent damage to individuals. The subordination of the Forces to the multiple safeguard system of the WHS, and its specialized training and equipment, makes it virtually impossible that its leaders could take power into their own hands and render the Forces independent of the system. Operating within the system, however, they can effectively prevent the upcropping of the "Hitler-problem" by commanding just enough deterrence capability to offset the power of a would-be aggressor.* The Forces are equipped according to plans worked out jointly by the Council of Principals and the Implementing Board, following policy-directives by the OSSC.

9.3 *World Economic System.* The WES carries out operations designed to realize optimum-states in the world economy. In an optimum-state, the inputs and outputs of capital are balanced at the limits of technological capacities and actual population size.

Balance in the world economy does not mean uniformity either with regard to economic practices or economic goals in local regions. Underdeveloped areas can continue to have economic growth, whereas highly developed regions may have to have negative growth rates with respect to certain key variables, such as energy and resource consumption. Hence a constant stock of world capital could allow the gradual equalization of economic standards, and the differential allocation of economic priorities. It is the sum of all locally differentiated processes that is of relevance.

If the sum of economic processes is an increase in capital

* It is assumed that by the year 2000 disarmament agreements will have been reached and implemented, reducing the nuclear stockpiles of the great powers. WHS deterrence capability will not be sufficient to impose a nuclear blackmail on the rest of the world, but merely to exceed the striking capacity of any given nation.

incommensurate with the existing population (as defined by the existing level of technological development), the WEM is directed to undertake measures to reduce capital investment. (The alternative measure to achieve stability is to increase depreciation; this however produces high turnover and therewith contributes to the depletion of raw materials and to higher levels of pollution.) Stabilizing economic processes at low rates of input and output is not the end of material progress, only its redirection from quantitative, material-consuming and pollution-generating factors to qualitative factors involving the longevity of goods and the availability of services. Competition between economic systems continues regardless of whether the systems operate on the principle of a corporate capitalist free market, or a state-owned or controlled economy. Economic patterns are set by the private or public management in accordance with local and regional needs, human and material resources, but with emphasis on low-investment and low-depreciation practices.

The World Economic System consists of two specialized subsystems: the informative Economic Advisory Service, and the authoritative Monetary and Tax Policy Council.

9.3.1 *The World Economic Advisory Service* evolves guidelines for economic development and dedevelopment in critical areas of the world economy. It is primarily concerned with capital-assistance programs for underdeveloped economies, and policy-guidance studies for superaffluent societies. Its services are in the area of relevant operational models for guiding economic development, wherever such guidance is necessary. It makes available detailed studies of the economic problems of a region and can send teams of experts to work with national governments in realigning economic practices to reduce actual or potential deviations from world economic optimum-states. Its services are required primarily in the under- and over-developed countries. The former have great need for economic development to alleviate human misery and assure adequate living standards, and the latter require assistance to assure selective dedevelopment for keeping energy and resource usage rates as well as pollution generation within acceptable thresholds. The Economic Advisory Service works out the indicated economic programs and assigns indicators with recommended dates of attainment. In the event of voluntary compliance with its suggested policies, the economies are expected to evolve along the lines suggested in the program. If, however, wide deviations occur, either through a sabotaging of the suggested guidelines or from unexpected factors, a more forceful intervention in the economic processes of the area is necessitated. This occurs through the World Monetary and Tax Policy Council.

9.3.2 *The World Monetary and Tax Policy Council* receives authorization from the Central Implementing Board, on instruction from the OSSC and the Council of Principals, to regulate the monetary reserves of a noncooperating or persistently stressing economic area and impose differentiated taxing and trade schedules. If continued growth is required in the area to raise living standards and literacy levels, and to alleviate misery, the flows of money and trade are temporarily facilitated, thereby stimulating economic and economy-dependent educational activity. If the economy exceeds standards compatible with global optimum-states, reverse measures depress the flow of money and impose trade restrictions (but leave open avenues of development in the areas of education, health, and other services; product longevity; and reduced capital depreciation).*

The operations of the World Monetary and Tax Policy

---

* Much as it runs counter to the growth-ideology of the past decades, "dedevelopment" will become a major challenge for economics, much as development has been in the past. When world-system consciousness crystallizes among the people of economically developed countries, economic growth-values will no longer be dominant, and hence selective dedevelopment toward a steady-state compatible with the world economy will no longer be perceived as the disaster that conservatives see in it today.

Council are activated when the economic data-gathering agencies report persistent mismatches with normal developmental pathways in an economy. If the affected actor feels that the fact of intervention itself is unjustified, it can file for review procedures with the OSPR Court. If on the other hand grievances arise out of the *manner* in which target operations are implemented, grievance procedures can be filed with the competent branch of the Executive Courts.

9.4 *World Population Council.* The task of the WPC is to help bring about a stable world population at a low level of input and output. Population is stable when the birth rate equals the death rate. This balance can be achieved at high as well as low rates. Commensurately with the universal valuation of longevity of life, the aim of the WPC is to stabilize world population at *low* birth and death rates. To accomplish this, the Council operates through two specialized agencies: the World Population Information Agency, and the World Health Organization. The function of the former is to decrease excessive birth rates, and of the latter to decrease excessive death rates.

9.4.1 *The World Population Information Agency* makes available information on population trends in all areas of the globe. It works with local governments to establish population norms for given areas, states, and regions. In accordance with the WHS's principle of noninterference with the basic political decisions of individual countries, governments set the population norms for their territories. Such norms entail commitments, however, for trends in other functional areas and represent compromises or trade-offs between growth objectives. For example, a larger population entails a lower average material standard of life measured in terms of per capita energy and raw material consumption, pollution generation, and capital investment in industry, and requires a larger food production. Any trade-off is acceptable in the light of the WHS's mandate for global homeostasis, provided it offers satisfactory modes of existence for the given population (a level above the poverty line) without stressing the global commons in the form of excessive consumption of resources, use of ocean or land, and pollution of air and waters.*

When local population norms are established, the WPIA objective is to bring about an adjustment of the birth rate corresponding to the norms through voluntary restrictions of family size. Two factors conjoin in determining the success of this process: a shift in public values and morality from high to low family size; and the availability of contraceptive devices. The Information Agency works through local public information media to raise the level of awareness of the seriousness of the population problem; and with local public health services to make available contraceptive devices and eliminate fears, as well as moral and religious scruples, hindering their use. A program of public education is worked out in collaboration with the educational institutions of the affected region. Where needed, financial assistance is channeled to these institutions through the Monetary and Tax Council. Informative and educational programs of family planning are initiated involving all stages, from contraception to abortion, with the final decision to make use of them left to individuals. Coercion beyond informative and educational techniques is not contemplated, as it conflicts with the principle of minimum interference with individual and national lifestyles and beliefs.

9.4.2 *The World Health Organization* (incorporating the present United Nations agency by that name) combats health problems that reduce average human life spans and increase the death rate. It does this through medical assistance, expansion of hospital facilities, training of physicians, and public education programs for healthier living. While efforts to re-

---

* Enforcement of this total "population package" prevents governments from setting excessively high population-growth rates (for example, as in Roumania in 1969 when the government went all out to raise fertility rates), while leaving the decision for the trade-offs in their hands.

duce the death rate are required in all areas of the world, priorities for assistance by the WHO are assigned in view of achieving a balance with the birth rate. Where the birth rate is high, the reduction of the death rate results in a population explosion. On the other hand, where the birth rate is low, or gives evidence of responding to informative and educational programs, an excessive death rate receives top WHO priority: reducing it helps to achieve a stable population. By assigning differential weightings to requests for its services, the WHO provides impetus to family planning and indirectly contributes to the success of the Population Information Agency's programs.

9.5 *World System for Ecological Balance.* The fourth executive branch of the WHS is designed to prevent the occurrence, and minimize the effects, of disasters and catastrophes resulting from the misuse and mismanagement of natural forces and relations in the global ecology.* It operates programs of public information favoring necessary changes in people's levels of ecological awareness, and conducts authoritative programs of intervention to prevent disasters and catastrophes. If such have already occurred, it operates a rescue program to reduce their impact. The overall goal of the World System for Ecological Balance is to safeguard the planet's ecology from pernicious intervention by corporations and governments, while allowing the proliferation of biodiversity and respecting the freedom of national and regional actors to pursue their own paths of sociocultural development.

The WSEB consists of three subsystems: the Ecological In-

---

* Following a suggestion by Anthony R. Michaels (in the *Bulletin of the Atomic Scientists*, April 1973, p. 24), we define accident as involving 1 to 1,000 people dead or in imminent danger of death; disaster as 1,000 to 1,000,000 people dead or in imminent danger of death, and catastrophe as more than 1,000,000 people dead or in imminent danger of death. The WHS does not concern itself with accidents, since normally adequate means for dealing with them are available locally; and it can deal with catastrophe effectively if it has sufficient advance notice to mobilize resources and personnel which exceed its normal operating capacity.

formation Agency, the Ecological Authority, and the Rescue Organization.

9.5.1 *The World Ecological Information Agency* is the informative and educational arm of the WSEB. It attempts to create a perception of the earth and its life processes as an estate to be prudently administered both for the benefit of the present occupants and for posterity, rather than as a heap of plunder waiting to be possessed and exploited by those who command the tools and techniques of technology.[3] To this end the Agency initiates large-scale public information programs, similar in scope and execution to the programs of the Population Information Agency, but specifically centering on the issues and ethics of ecological balance. If a strong bias exists toward voluntarism, and grassroots support is available, the efforts of the Agency are directed to identifying the crucial issues and the sensitive points of the political, economic, and technological systems where reforms can be introduced through increasing consensus regarding need. The agency's goal is to activate participatory governance in matters of ecological balance, rather than constraints to assure such balance by authoritative directives. It serves as a clearing house for information on all matters pertaining to the environment, including quality standards, reserves of nonrenewable raw materials, harvesting of as yet untapped resources, wildlife conservation, and potential sources of danger such as the melting of the polar icecaps, large-scale pollution, and hazards due to poisonous or unstable substances (such as the storage and dumping of radioactive wastes).

9.5.2 *The World Ecological Authority* is the authoritative executive agency of the WHS in the area of ecological balance. Its main task is to survey the usage of nonrenewable natural resources which are essential for the sustenance of life anywhere on the globe. This applies especially to platinum, mercury, oil, copper, phosphorus, some exotic metals, and gold. In this category come also the resources represented by

A STRATEGY FOR THE FUTURE

the oceans and the atmosphere. In addition, the Authority acts to prevent ecodisasters or catastrophes, of both technologic and natural origin. Its mandate is to carry out its regulative functions with minimum interference with economic and ecologic diversity. The Authority's operations may be enforced by the World Security Forces, when so directed by the OSSC.

9.5.3 *The World Rescue Organization* consists of a network of supply depots and regional coordinating offices, with access to adequate personnel to handle ecodisasters (i.e., events with between 1,000 and 1,000,000 dead, or in imminent danger of death). Whereas the Ecological Authority is mainly concerned with the control of ecological balance and prevention of disasters, the Rescue Organization is there to minimize their effects. The WRO receives data from the World Ecology Monitor via special high-speed channels, alerts rescue personnel, determines the needs for supplies and their location relative to the disaster area, and mounts the rescue operation with optimum efficiency.

The World Rescue Organization deals with two kinds of disasters: natural, and technological. Natural disasters may be induced by such phenomena as earthquakes, thunderstorms, floods, and tidal waves. While these are independent of the accelerated pace of human societal development, their effects increase proportionately to population density, and the degree to which populations rely on technological means for existence. Essential technologies may be damaged by natural events, and cause further damage themselves (e.g., storm-induced crashes of giant planes, earthquake-induced breakdowns of dams, destruction of containers of hazardous materials. Such disasters are likely to increase in frequency with population growth and the worldwide availability of high-power technology. They will occur through human error, insufficient safety precautions, or from unforeseen accidents. They can produce anomalies in nuclear power stations with radioactive fallout, fires, the accidental activation of stockpiled nuclear arms (even if these are restricted to deterrence use by a peace-enforcing world agency), and drastic pollutions of the oceans, rivers, or the atmosphere. Technological advance brings with it the increased probability of technological accidents, and possibly disasters. Their effects are unlikely to be confined to one country, and their handling thus requires a supranational rescue operation. This the WRO is designed to provide.

9.6 *The Circuit Fuses = The Executive Grievance System.* Three specialized courts operate within the Executive Grievance System. They process grievances arising from the actions of the three specialized executive agencies that have mandates to intervene in the affairs of regional and national actors when so directed by the WHS decision-makers. (These agencies are the World Security Forces, the World Monetary and Tax Policy Council, and the World Ecological Authority.)

9.6.1 *The World Security Court* provides for review of the actions of the World Security Forces when requests for such procedures are filed by regional or national actors. The Court's first task is to establish whether legitimate grounds for grievance exist. If this is found to be the case, the Court undertakes corrective measures in keeping with the sense of the directives which motivated the action of the Security Forces. The Court has no power to modify the OSSC decision which called for the intervention under review, but limits itself to examining the legitimacy of the action taken, in the light of the existing directives. If the Court finds that the directive cannot be implemented without provoking some grievances, it appeals to the Optimum-State Policy Review Court. If that Court upholds the directive, the World Security Court is competent to decide on the legitimacy of the grievances arising out of its mode of implementation.

9.6.2. *The World Monetary and Tax Policy Court* has analogous tasks and responsibilities. It reviews grievances arising from the actions of the World Monetary and Tax Policy Council and establishes whether they relate to implementation procedures or to the decisions being implemented. If the former, it has competence to reach a binding decision. If the latter, it appeals to the OSPR Court for final decision. Further grievances in the case are then decided on the basis of whether or not the OSPR Court upholds the original OSSC directive.

9.6.3 *The World Ecology Court* handles grievances in connection with the actions of the World Ecological Authority. It proceeds in a manner precisely analogous to the other two Executive Courts within its own area of competence.

If grievances are filed with more than one court simultaneously, as resulting from a compound effect of the actions of more than one authoritative executive agency, the Courts sit in joint session. Cases for which no constitutional guidelines exist are brought to the OSPR Court for decision.


# A Scenario for Transition

(i)  *Steps*

Step 1. *Global-level decision-makers negotiate a blueprint for the constitution of the World Homeostat System.* Approximately a decade of the ecofeedback information-decision flow among the world's peoples brings into sharp focus the need to master trends which affect the security and well-being of mankind. Decisions passed between the levels of town-hall meetings, from the neighborhood to the global, bring forth a multitude of resolutions, trade-offs, modifications, and improvements designed in view of the long-term goal of creating a global organization for the effective handling of processes vital to the human future. The global-level policy-making structure is entrusted with opening the negotiations. This body—which may be the United Nations General Assembly, a special organization called into life by it, or a successor—

begins consultations with the pertinent global-level organizations. These include some which already exist at the time of writing, such as the World Bank; some which are just coming into being, for example, the World Population Society; and others which are postulated for a later phase, e.g., the integrated information source of the late twentieth century.

Negotiations concern the integration of the functions of the existing global functional actors in a coordinated actor which carries out a joint mandate of the world's peoples. The actor is to incorporate the ecofeedback information source and data-gathering organization and couple it with an executive capability derived from the coordinated operation of the global functional actors, endowed with sufficient power and authority to satisfy the mandate. The first phases of negotiation establish the basic mandate in the form of the goals of the new world organization. These refer to the four essential functional areas of world security, economy, ecology, and population, and specify global conditions which combine long-term tenability with genuine humanism. Minimum standards of life are established in reference to a hierarchy of human needs, and the socially mediated resources and conditions capable of its satisfaction. The rights of individuals, organizations, nation-states, multinational, international, and regional actors are defined in relation to the equitable distribution of the goods, services, and institutional patterns required to meet the demands of human need-fulfillment on all principal levels, with especial attention to the basic needs for survival, safety, and group-belongingness.

The rights of individual and collective actors also include the right to protection from any actor that threatens to thwart or constrain their conditions of need-fulfillment. As interference with individual action is legitimized (on Mill's principle) when a person's conduct affects prejudicially the interests of others, and these others have a right of protection by society, so in the new world law interference with the actions of any constituted social system is legitimized when that system prejudices the interests of others in the world community. The world community as such is committed to protecting all systems from the prejudicial activities of any offender. The concept of legitimate interference with the activities of nation-states, as the protection of the rights of all states (and regions formed by states), constitutes the legal foundation for the WHS; it is a foundation based on the extension of the rights and responsibilities of states to the global level, corresponding to the expansion—by the end of the century—of the general level of social and political consciousness.

The first step ends with an operational blueprint for the constitution of the World Homeostat System (although its real-world name is likely to be more poetic, if less descriptive). Its charter is signed by the representatives of the global-level policy-making body established in the previous decade. The signatures carry the affirmation and agreement of all participating national governments.

Step 2. *The work of implementation begins, and continues until the WHS is fully operative.* Implementation involves three basic elements: funding, personnel, and physical plants.

Funding of the WHS is assured through the graduated taxation system of national, corporate, and individual actors outlined previously, and administered by the functional components of the WHS (i.e., the World Revenue Service and the World Treasury). Prior to the creation of these components, special committees are appointed by the global-level policy-makers to collect and administer funds necessary to implement the projects. Funding needs are communicated through the existing ecofeedback information channels and discussed at each level of town-hall meeting. Resolutions passed from level to level respond to needs in the light of their perceived justification as measured by the mandated constitution of the WHS. Initial funds are allocated by the special committees to the separate tasks of identifying and engaging the personnel of the various WHS components, and acquiring the physical plants necessary for operation.

The personnel needs of the WHS are most stringent: they call for executives in all departments who are free of the bias of national or regional interests. Persons dedicated to the human good supranationally may exist only in small numbers at the time of writing and, beyond international civil servants, may not include a significant number of persons qualified for executive positions. But between the present and the postulated time of implementation of the WHS projects lies a period of several decades, during which previous phases of strategy contribute to the raising of world-system consciousness in all societies and at all socioeconomic levels. As at any previous time in history, when national sentiments and goals crystallized there arose figures who could represent them, transcending the accidents of their particular place of origin and values of upbringing, so there will be personalities emerging from the world's peoples who will be capable of representing universal human interests when global awareness has reached the required level. These people will be increasingly active in policy-making and begin to influence domestic political structures decades earlier. When the tasks of implementation begin, they will be known on their respective levels of active involvement and can be recruited for offices corresponding to their abilities.

Selection criteria for WHS executives will be a composite of two factors: proven dedication to the human good beyond provincial and national bias, and competence for carrying out specific responsibilities. The top executives of each functional component of the WHS will be selected by personnel committees appointed by the global-level policy-makers directly; further personnel will be nominated by the executives and screened by the committees. The bureaucracy of the WHS can thus be assembled from the top down, in hierarchical steps, controlled by the application of uniform criteria for unbiased dedication and specialized competence.

Acquisition of the physical plants of the system can begin when the major executives of each branch have been recruited and revenues can be systematically collected and allocated. Working in temporary headquarters, the executives of the World Treasury work out allocation schedules for the approval of the OSSC members. Budgets for the various components are established, and the process of the implementation of the housing and equipment needs of the system begins. Channels for feedback and review, built into the operating procedures of the WHS, provide for corrections for mistakes in planning and modification in the act of construction. Shells to house the administrative bureaucracies are constructed first: here the selection of sites and the hardware for intercommunication among the units involves the most painstaking planning. Secondly, the specialized equipment of the functional components is acquired: computers, information-gathering networks, information-disseminating networks, equipment for the rescue organization and the security forces. The minimal nuclear arms capability of the latter required to overcome any single potential aggressor constitutes the most difficult step, since it involves the voluntary surrender of military supremacy by powerful national actors. It may be the last step in the implementation of the WHS project.

When it commands the necessary revenues, dedicated and competent personnel, and operational equipment, the WHS begins its work as the historically first organization to watch over and effectively safeguard the collective interests of all the world's peoples.

(ii) *Time*

Working within the increasingly fuzzy time horizons of the third and final phase of this strategy, we can discern some general time-thresholds which appear reasonable from the perspective of the present. The threshold for the first step of this phase appears to be the year 2000 on the near, and 2020 on the far side. It is unlikely that sufficient momentum could be gathered through the ecofeedback information-decision process prior to 2000 to lead to realistic negotiations in view of producing an operational blueprint for the WHS; and if that information-decision process is unable to crystallize sufficient consensus to bring about such negotiations by 2020, it is unlikely to gather such momentum later. Failure could be ascribed, optimistically, to a process of mutual international and interregional accommodation which makes further measures superfluous; and it could be ascribed pessimistically to a breakdown of consensus over emerging conflicts of interest, which precludes that negotiations get off the ground.

The subphase of negotiations could last anywhere from one year to a decade. The complexity of the issues seems to forbid an estimate shorter than a single year; and the loss of momentum entailed by negotiations extended over an entire decade precludes the likelihood that they could be successfully concluded beyond that time-span. Within these thresholds, the decisive factor is the level of commitment and feeling of urgency that the parties bring to the negotiating table. These in turn depend both on degrees of trauma brought about by such processes as population pressures, economic competition and inequality, deterioration of the environment, the arms race and threat of confrontation, dwindling natural and food resources, and worldwide energy crises, and on the conviction of national and regional decision-makers that the problems can and must be resolved through supranational cooperation. In general, the higher the level of trauma, the higher the degree of perceived urgency, and the more motivated—and therefore the more efficient and hence shorter—the negotiations.

Thus we get 2001 as the earliest (and unlikely) threshold

for the negotiation subphase, and 2030 as the latest threshold. The implementation of the negotiated decisions is likewise conditioned by the above factors, and could take anywhere from a period of a few years to several decades. It is unrealistic to contemplate the beginning of World Homeostat operations prior to the first decade of the twenty-first century, and it is entirely possible to envisage it at almost anytime until mid-century. For periods beyond that time-span our present horizons become increasingly vague, and we pass from reasoned forecasts based on past and present trends to the realm of pure speculation.

# GLOBAL HOMEOSTASIS: AN EVALUATION OF THE MEANS AND THE ENDS

The time has come to take stock of our findings and proposals. We can do so by first briefly summarizing the nature of the societal need today and the manner in which the proposed strategies seek to satisfy it, and then evaluating the predicted outcome in reference to means as well as to ends.

## Toward Global Homeostasis

### 1. The Need

Development in complex systems proceeds by building hierarchical sequences of levels of stability, each endowed with its own dynamics and regulatory potentials. The next level to be reached in human societal development is that of the world system. It has already been reached in the functional areas which normally motivate change and act as the mainspring of evolution. However, our societal technics of dealing with the global level of organization lag behind. Due to the application of nation-state–centered provincial ideas and technics, the growth of the functional trends goes unchecked and threatens to unbalance the system, depressing the chances and conditions of human life. In order to maintain an optimum carrying capacity for humanity on the planet, supranational societal technics have to be evolved to effectively stabilize functional growth trends at the optimum level defined by our technological capacity to manage our environment. Failure to do so will incur increasing stresses and could trigger any one of a number of different catastrophes, ranging from ecocatastrophes to overcrowding, famine, epidemics, and thermonuclear wars.

## The Strategies of Meeting the Need

### 2. *The Strategy*

*Phase one: the era of world-system consciousness.* From a nucleus of already globally thinking individuals, such as international civil servants, social and natural scientists and students, corporate managers, professional people, and people in the arts and in public media, concern and discussion radiates outwards, entraining a rising level of consciousness first among the counterculture and opposition and reform groups, later among the wider strata of citizens. Rising levels of discussion entrain in turn greater attention by the public media, and prompt the influx of world-systemically thinking people in the domestic and international political arena.

*Phase two: the era of multilevel decisions.* The rise of popular consensus to world-system levels prompts major governments to seek continued support through adequate responses. These include the creation of a supranational information source with a global network of dissemination, producing a constant flow of updated information on current trends and patterns, alternative solutions, and the effect of previous solutions on the process. The subsequent creation of a multilevel political participation system, operating both within and among individual nation-states, channels the forming consensus on specific issues and policies toward concrete realization. Decisions percolate from the grass-roots level upwards, become modified in the light of constraints apparent at each level, and get implemented in multiple layers. Their effect is communicated to the next round of multiechelon decision-making, and, in successive runs, measures are taken to correct for overshoots, undershoots, mistaken targets, and neglected objectives.

*Phase three: the era of global homeostasis.* The most probable result of the multiechelon decision and information operations is the crystallization of a perceived need for a universal functional actor to regulate critical trends in the world system. Under the continued impact of the consensus and decision-formation process, national governments agree to jointly constitute an impartial universal actor entrusted with specific regulatory tasks. The creation of this actor constitutes the addition of a self-regulative mechanism to the world system, rendering it dynamically stable around desirable optimum-states. Societal technics now match and are able to handle material technics, and humanity has entered the era of global homeostasis.

## Evaluation of the Means

### 1. *Rationality*

The first question with which we must confront the proposal of a World Homeostat System is this: Is it intrinsically reasonable? Can cybernetic concepts furnish a scheme applicable to vast societal processes?

When pondering this question, we should note that although modern cybernetics grew out of engineering rather than social and political philosophy, analogous concepts have a long history of application in the social realm. The word itself derives from the Greek *kybernetes* which means guide or pilot. It was used by Plato to describe the prudential aspect of the art of governing; in modern times, Ampère spoke of *la cybernétique* to indicate the science of government. The Latin term *gubernator* is the root for the English word "governor," with the latter used both to denote the head of certain political organizations and the speed-control mechanism in steam engines. Wiener himself, who resuscitated the term "cybernetics," argued that the operation of the living individual and the operation of some of the newer communication machines are precisely parallel. He did not exclude society either, as he made amply clear in a book tellingly entitled *The Human Use of Human Beings: Cybernetics and Society* (1950).

In the 1960s and early 1970s an increasing number of social scientists turned to cybernetic concepts in their analyses of social and political systems. The cogency of their approach rests on the observation that, regardless of whether we consider an artificial control system, a living organism, or a sociopolitical system, we find that they exhibit (1) goal parameters set in a control center, (2) sensing mechanisms whereby information relevant to the system's goals is registered in the system, (3) effector mechanisms whereby the system acts on its environment, and (4) transformation rules or procedures whereby information received from the sensors is compared with information about the goal states, and an error-correcting signal is produced to modify the behavior of the effectors. The function of correcting for deviations from the paths of goal-attainment is that of the central regulator. It must contain a long-term memory which stores the system's norms, i.e., the goal-conditions which the system pursues by means of its deviation-reducing behavior.

Yet the cybernetic analysis of complex human systems poses serious difficulties for the investigator. Such systems have not only mechanisms characterized by stereotyped functions (such as functional agencies and bureaucracies with clearly defined objectives and procedures) but also manifest a large residue of "fuzzy" dynamics where centers of function and influence form and reform under the operation of some general principle deriving from the situation of the whole system in view of its internal or external constraints.* For this reason an organic systems approach to sociocultural and political systems is more fruitful than the more narrow (if also more rigorous) cybernetic approach. However, the problems which beset the cybernetic analysis of complex real-world sociocultural and political systems do not confront the problem of *designing* a functional guidance system. This is basically an engineering task in which we can be clear about objectives, constraints, as well as functions. We can specify the feedback loops between the components, and entrust specific tasks to specific actors. Sensing, decision-making, implementing, information storing and retrieving, as well as coordinating and supervising, can be outlined without the fuzziness associated with real-world systems which, like Topsy, were not born but just grew. Hence the design for a global guidance system can benefit from cybernetic principles, even if the application of such principles in the analysis of existing complex sociocultural systems faces serious difficulties.

## 2. *Efficiency*

Even if we satisfy ourselves that a cybernetic design for regulating complex societal processes is intrinsically reasonable, we must still ask whether the particular design outlined here is the optimal one. Obviously, it would be foolish to claim that it is the best possible cybernetic design for a global functional regulator; the much more modest claim indicated is that it is but a first approximation. Yet even if a long series

* See "Systemic Invariance," The section on Self–Stabilization, in the *Appendix*, below.

of refinements were undertaken and in the end we were confronted with a totally new design, we could still test this particular model for functional efficiency in its role as a basis for refinement. Such testing can be perfected through the techniques of computer simulation and game theory. Alternative scenarios can be designed with specific types and sequences of problems and constraints, and players simulating roles within the system asked to respond to them. Numerical values may be assigned to global optimum-states, as well as to initial conditions characterizing the parameters when the testing begins. The various aspects of system performance may be quantified, and time factors involved in decision-making, implementation, and in the communication of information among the components can be taken into account. Degrees of difficulty can be associated with achieving various goals in view of formal or informal resistance in the system's environment. "Optimum–State Games" can then be played with the model, testing its efficiency as an instrument for resolving problems, as well as the players' skill in producing the adequate responses.

For the present, we shall content ourselves with a preliminary, qualitative testing of the design. This can be done in the same terms we would use to investigate any control system's efficiency, i.e., in reference to load, lag, gain, and lead.[1] Depending on the likelihood that the system can perform well with respect to these factors, we can estimate its performance on a scale ranging from poor to excellent.

The test questions are the following:

i. What are the operational tasks of the system in reaching the target conditions? The answer defines the system's *load*.

ii. How much time does the system take to process information between the point of entry in its sensors and the output point in the effectors? This question concerns itself with *lag*.

iii. How effective are the responses produced by the system in terms of approaching and eventually reaching its target? This specifies the system's *gain*.

iv. Is there a significant amount of anticipation of conditions relevant to reaching the target in the decision centers of the system? The answer defines the system's *lead*.

LOAD. The World Homeostat System's load is defined by the degree of difficulty inherent in converting an unstable, growth-oriented world system into a stable, optimum-state system by regulating critical processes in the four relevant functional areas. At this time the dimension of this load is not known, and can only be guessed. It is clear, on the other hand, that provisions for handling it as competently as the state of current knowledge permits are built into the WHS in the form of multidisciplinary research and integrating boards equipped with long-term memory-stores, and having access to up-to-date empirical information. The principal such organ is constituted as the Special and General Panels of the Research Boards operating in association with the Optimum–State Steering Committee. The Boards are in a better position to assess relevant global trends than any real-world organization in history. They have access to information gathered by specialized monitors switched into global information networks and integrated by competent panels; they have at their command the feasibility studies of the specialized research boards associated with the Council of Principals, and can draw on the computerized storage and retrieval system operated by each WHS agency including the General Secretariat. The chances are thus maximized that the WHS policies are based on complete and accurate data, have a desirable intent, and are feasible to carry out. Hence even if the exact magnitude of the load cannot be assessed from the vantage point of the present, and although we guess that it is considerable, we can say that the WHS is optimally equipped to handle it. It commands the information gathering, processing, storing, and retrieving facilities commensurate with the task to the best of the available human and technological capabilities.

LAG. The World Homeostat System is designed to process information according to the basic prototype of a simple control system. There are no superfluous loops or dead-ends in the flow from sensor to regulator, to correlator, and to effector. Additional components are switched in to assure safety, such as input and output monitors and the "fuses" represented by the OSPR and the Executive Courts. As always, there is a trade-off between minimizing lag and maximizing security. Lag can be further cut by feeding information from the sensor agencies directly to the top decision-making bodies and from there directly to the executive organs. However, such procedure might allow items of information to be missed, others to be overemphasized, and decisions to be handed down without further scrutiny of their validity, and have as a consequence operations that produce side-effects which increase, rather than reduce, the load on the system. Hence the problem is not to eliminate, but to reduce lag to the minimum compatible with safe operation. In general, we can say that any system that conforms to the basic information-flow design of a simple control system has no superfluous elements that introduce lag; and one that contains additional elements only in the immediate interests of safe operation produces only a minimum desirable lag. Whether a further reduction of lag could be effected in the WHS without impairing the margin of safety in its operations is an empirical question, calling for actual experience with the operation of the system. It could also be, conversely, that experience would call for additional safety loops in the system. If such loops were introduced, lag would increase in absolute quantity but would still conform to the concept of minimum desirable lag.

GAIN. The WHS is designed for maximum gain without overshoot. The elements assuring such performance are the separate operating channels of the sensor and the effector, and the multiple research and monitoring boards. Specialized monitors switched into global information networks in the key areas of ecology, population, economy, and world security assure that information is available to the system with optimum speed. Likewise, specialized effectors home in on specified targets with maximum efficiency. The correlation of the four sets of sensors and effectors through a minimum-lag decision process assures overall speed of operation combined with specialized efficiency. Possible side-effects of specialty blindfolds are eliminated by the integration of data at the input level (by the World Information Coordinating Board), as well as by the dissection of decisions according to specialized competences immediately prior to implementation (by the Implementing Board). Hence, although the sensors and effectors of the system are specialized, the decision-making process deals with integrated information. Optimum conditions are thereby obtained for efficient system response. Provided the functional organs do their job, high gain should result without overshoot. Prevention of the latter is one of the tasks of the Research Boards of the OSSC, where the Special and General Panels analyze information and update long-term maps of real-world conditions. Thus unilateral action, designed to attain a target condition without regard to its possible side-effects on other aspects of the target configuration, or even on the same aspect in the future, is not likely to occur.

LEAD. To what extent the WHS can predict future conditions depends on the sum of knowledge and applied expertise of its research boards. At the present time, predictions of long-term processes are based on the constancy of the essential dynamics by which the variables are correlated, e.g., the growth of population is projected on the basis of the constancy of human reproductive patterns on given levels of material and social existence, and economic growth processes are projected on the basis of the constancy of consumer and investor behavior under similarly identifiable recurrent conditions. Short-term predictions do not greatly suffer from our ignorance of the changing dynamics of human behavior, but long-term predictions are mostly reduced to guesswork. However, experience with the manipulation of a large range of variables over time should provide the foundation for better techniques of prediction. Developing predictive models of a humanistic world order is the responsibility of the Research Boards. If their models are sufficiently expert, the decisions of the OSSC basically sound, and the feasibility reports reliable, a significant amount of lead can be introduced into the operations.

A perfect system would be fully predictive and could undertake measures to prevent any deviations before they could occur. However, striving for such predictive capability is not realistic. We must content ourselves with a limited capacity for lead, and some finite reduction of lag; i.e., with an error-*corrective* rather than an error-*preventive* system.

## Evaluation of the Ends

Even if we claim that global homeostasis is the necessary cure for the ills of our times, we can still question its intrinsic desirability. Is the cure really better than the illness? Will life be worth living under conditions of global homeostasis?

We must face the conditions which emerge whenever a developmental process comes to an end, is leveled off, and is stabilized. The end of progress is a discouraging state. Must we accept it as the inevitable destiny of human civilization?

Critics of the zero-growth ideas are quick to point to the dangers of societal stagnation. They tell us that ZEG (Zero Economic Growth) transforms economic processes into a zero-sum game: in a stationary economy, what one man gains another must lose. This contrasts with the rosier picture of a growth economy, where the rich can become richer without the poor becoming poorer, and where it pays more to exploit new inventions and natural resources than each other, so that social conflict is diminished. In a no-growth economy personal-growth efforts in the pertinent dimensions directly increase conflict: material growth can be achieved only through the redistribution of a constant stock of capital, i.e., through exploitation of persons by persons or classes by classes. In order to regulate such conflicts, a mafia-type authority structure is required, or else a convincing ideology of equality. The former is undesirable, and the latter, unrealistic. Moreover there is no "safety valve" in a stationary state, no place where the discontented, nonconformist, or overly ambitious could be discharged. There is no longer an America as an open continent for the adventurous and the poor of Europe; no longer even an American West for the similar segment of the settled American population. There is no escape from the zero-sum economy when economic growth is halted globally.

The other principal dimension of a no-growth society presents an equally dismal picture. ZPG (Zero Population Growth) produces an undesirably top-heavy age distribution, approximating a Florida retirement colony. In the long run age balance would be reestablished through replacement-value fertility, with about equal numbers of people in all age groups up to the level of average life expectancy. But replacement-level fertility is premised either on external coercion (rigorous birth-control measures with economic, social, and legal penalties) or voluntary compliance. The former presupposes the mafia-type structure of ZEG, and the latter a sufficient level of understanding and value adaptation. If the understanding and value adaptation is unevenly distributed, those who possess it will phase themselves out, whereas the irresponsible people who disregard or fail to comprehend the call for ZPG will breed undisturbed. Within a few generations only their offspring would populate the globe. Further population regulations would then have to rely on coercion— unless the children of irresponsible parents can be socially reeducated, a process which pitches social values firmly against family values and has slim chances of succeeding.

ZEG as well as ZPG resolves problems only to create new ones. The growth ills of contemporary society would be replaced by the ills of a totalitarian structure dedicated to enforcing a stationary state. Whereas life may become impossible if growth continues unchecked, it may become not worth living if growth is brutally leveled off. The alternatives are not pleasing. Fortunately, these are not true alternatives but merely two out of a number of different pathways, some of which provide happier perspectives.

A global homeostasis defined in reference to complex, both regionally and temporally variable, steady-states is such a preferable pathway. The optimum-state which the WHS is to maintain through the principle of minimum interference with the political principles and domestic affairs of societies is not a stationary state, arbitrarily frozen at a given level. It is, rather, a state defined by humanistic global conditions, i.e., global parameters which jointly enable the human population to fulfill its hierarchy of needs. This state is

    (i)  partially changing,
    (ii)  never fully attained,
    (iii)  a variable yet enduring goal of human striving.

Changes of the optimum-state are prompted both by real-world conditions (such as changes in population growth and composition, discoveries of new energy sources and sinks, pollution-reduction capacities, raw-material conversion processes, distribution techniques, etc.) and by conceptual innovations (e.g., filling in of data-gaps, more precise models of economic and ecologic processes, and so on). No optimum-state is fully attained within any foreseeable time horizon, for initial conditions are sufficiently different, and societal processes sufficiently slow, not to bring about a normative world before our understanding of the normative world itself changes. Thus striving toward the optimum-state is like hunting a prey without ever catching it. Yet in this case the positive features are all associated with the hunt: it is what supplies motivation, and the incentive for innovation and creativity. As Dewey emphasized and humanistic psychologists constantly reaffirm, people require objective goals toward which they can strive and which they can progressively approach, rather than states of saturation where the goals are achieved and there is nothing more left to do. The good is in the seeking, not in final possession.

We should not conclude from this that the future motivation of mankind will consist of seeking an elusive, imperfectly defined and hence always changing condition. If the optimum-state could never be captured, striving toward it would seem to be as unsatisfying as hunting a prey that turns into a mirage as soon as it is approached. But there will be enduring determinations of the optimum-state, and successive modifications of changing elements would not negate the value of having striven for superseded determinations. A reduction in population growth-rates is likely to be an enduring feature of optimum-states for some time to come, and the husbanding of finite resources, though their relevance may change in time, is not likely to turn out to have been wasted effort. It is also possible to *attain* some determinations of the optimum-state (even if not the full constellation) before they change. Pollution levels can be reduced to absorption levels with improvements in techniques, higher investment in installing the devices, and rerouting the relevant dynamics of regional economies. World-security standards can be met through disarmament agreements and supranational supervising and control organs. Moving toward any of these objectives will not turn out to be futile even when our understanding of the exact nature of a global optimum-state undergoes modification.

Efforts to rechannel human motivation to seek higher levels of need-fulfillment in the cognitive and aesthetic domains will likewise prove to be enduring values of life under conditions of global homeostasis. The refinement of the entire range of human need-fulfillment will continue to pose challenges which are not invalidated within any foreseeable period. If there is room for creativity on a small, man-made spaceship, how much more room there is for creativity, ingenuity, and innovation on earth, with its complex natural and societal orders which we are only now beginning to comprehend!

The normative state of global homeostasis is not a stationary state, but a quasi-stationary, multivariable steady-state. It is not likely to frustrate human motivation, for the rules of zero-sum games do not apply. The success of one need not be paid for by the failure of another. Even material growth can continue in all areas where technologic invention makes better use of resources and produces more access to energies and raw materials. Yet growth by accretion, typical of material growth, is but one variety of growth and not the only one that is capable of offering a real challenge and an acceptable ideal to human beings. (Not that an accretion-type growth has a necessarily positive meaning: cancer is a good counterexample.) Growth in the refinement of the techniques of sociocultural life, in the improvement of social organization, in the distribution of goods and services, the accessibility of amenities, the reduction of external disamenities, and in the quality of human experience as mediated by art, science, religion, and even mysticism, are examples of positive growth although they have no necessary material accretion features. Nonzero-sum games will continue to be played in all areas of human need-fulfillment. Progress will not lose its meaning, or become attainable only at the expense of a compensating regress.

The operation of the WHS is designed to pinpoint areas of progress and channel human motivation toward realistically achievable need-fulfillments. If it succeeds, its policies will not appear arbitrary, undesirable, or irrational and will not require coercive enforcement.

A great deal of plasticity can be maintained within the world system if its basic goal-settings can be focused on the proper objectives. Such cannot be done in today's parochial and divisive world, with its largely material and population-growth–oriented dynamics. But in about three decades the picture could change, if processes similar to the consciousness-raising and multilevel decision-making strategies of the previous phases can unfold. A global perspective is the precondition of global regulation, much as the national perspective has been the precondition of the functioning of nation-states. When a global perspective is achieved, the institutional pinpointing and channeling of world-systemic development becomes not only a possibility: it becomes a broadly perceived *desideratum*. Its alternative, international aimlessness and anarchy, will be seen to be as abhorrent as the lack of order and goals in any smaller-scale society. And when the achievement of the necessary conditions of human need-fulfillment become the basis of societal motivation, attaining and maintaining a world order conducive to satisfactions will offer an enduring and meaningful challenge for creativity and innovation.

## Beyond the World Homeostat System

We can treat vaster time horizons axiomatically, if not empirically. We no longer engage in strategies based on forecasts of reasonable possibilities of policy decisions, but in assessments of the abstract possibilities inherent in a given situation. The situation of interest in this concluding section is that which comes about if and when the World Homeostat System is implemented. Have we reached the end of sociocultural evolution, or is this but a transitory phase as well?

Independently of whether or not the WHS will be implemented, and whether or not once implemented it will perpetuate itself, it is clear that there are no constraints inherent in its organization which would make it a frozen ultimate phase of sociocultural organization. It is a functional system created in view of certain emerging problems, and it is designed to handle such problems inasmuch as they persist and insofar as it is capable of doing so. In other words, the performance, and in fact the very existence of the WHS, is geared to its load. According to its mandate, if no load, no system. But as long as there is a load, the system's gain (efficiency in pursuing its ends) must be commensurate with the size of the load. Hence the more load, the greater the operating capacity of the system.

These are axiomatic propositions, not real-world forecasts. But they help us sort out the possibilities introduced by the creation of a WHS-type organization.

The axiomatic possibilities are these. (1) The system's load increases (e.g., as a result of progressively more acute conflicts, worsening problems, uncooperative behavior by national and regional actors). Then: (1a) the WHS's operating capacity increases commensurately; or (1b) the system's operations break down. (2) The system's load decreases (e.g., because of less acute conflicts, more localized or superficial problems, more cooperation by national and regional actors). Then: (2a) the WHS's operating capacity decreases commensurately, or (2b) it remains at the previous level ("overkill").

Possibility (1a) conduces in the direction of a world government commanding vast powers of coercion. (1b) leads to international anarchy and all the dangers inherent in it (essentially, a regress to the situation of the present but confronted with the conditions prevailing in the next century). (2a) brings about a process which, if sustained, could lead to gradually phasing out the WHS; and (2b) represents a nonfunctional self-perpetuation, at least for a limited time.

Of these abstract possibilities, (2a) is clearly the preferable. It is premised, however, on a decreasing load, and therewith on positive effects brought about by the system's operations. Pursuing the abstract scenario of (2a), we may envisage positive effects of WHS policies in the key areas of world security, economy, ecology, and population, resulting in more stable and humanistic conditions of existence for a population itself stabilized at a manageable global level. Lessening tensions reinforce the values and behavior patterns leading to them; international and interregional cooperation is assured through the enculturation of globally-oriented humanistic values. The role of the WHS becomes that of a coordinator and surveillant of spontaneously adaptive regional dynamics; its authoritative agencies are kept in abeyance and reserved for emergency functions.

The optimum long-term scenario foresees a world order where human needs are adequately satisfied. The greatest number of persons find the highest levels of satisfaction, thanks to the equitable distribution of resources that represent the necessary, if not sufficient, conditions for fulfillment of the hierarchy of human needs. Such distribution is achieved with the minimum of coercion and the highest humanly attainable degree of voluntary cooperation between individuals and groups. This, truly, is the route to paradise on earth. There is no assurance that it will be taken; we can merely point to its possibility in the wake of the institutionalization of the WHS. Global homeostasis *can* be humanistic without coercion.

But the road beyond a world authority to regulate the trends which presently threaten humanity on this planet cannot be realistically forecast. Perhaps we should rest content with the abstract possibility of a humanistic continuation, and strive for the more immediate objectives which conduce toward an acceptable and stable world order.

*Appendix*

# A REVIEW OF THE
# RELEVANT HYPOTHESES OF
# GENERAL SYSTEMS THEORY *

## The Evolution of Complexity

Evolutionary thinking is characteristic of process metaphysics, and of the newer theories of the empirical sciences. But whereas process metaphysics saw evolution as a cosmic process, embracing all empirical phenomena in a continuous if specifically differentiated sweep, the modern empirical sciences evolved special laws of evolution, applicable only within limited domains. Thus there is a law of the evolution of matter in the universe, stated in the equations of astrophysics; there is a law of the evolution of the macrostructure of the universe itself, based on the calculations of astronomy; there is also a law of the evolution of biological entities from macromolecules and protocells with replicating capability to complex and integrated multicellular organisms; there are other laws applicable to the evolution of ecosystems, still

* Nobody can speak in the name of an entire field without fear of contradiction. These hypotheses are derived from the author's work in the general systems area over the past several years; through his various publications, they have now entered the accepted literature of the field. This, however, does not preclude the possibility that some general systems theorists disagree with them. (For a more detailed presentation, see Ervin Laszlo, *Introduction to Systems Philosophy*, Part One. New York: Harper Torchbooks, 1973.)

others to sociocultural evolution (the controversial "laws of history"), and laws or principles of the evolution of science, art, and religion. The unitary vision of a continuous evolutionary process is upheld only by metaphysicians, divorced from the main streams of scientific thought.

Thanks to the rise of the systems sciences, however, general systems theory can now reaffirm the concept of a continuous, if internally highly differentiated, evolutionary process on a scientific basis. Its concept of evolution is the offspring of two initially opposing currents of thought within nineteenth-century science. One was the Darwinian theory of the origin of species; the other, the early formulations of the laws of thermodynamics.

In 1862 Spencer argued that there is a fundamental law of matter, called the law of persistence of force, from which it follows that nothing homogeneous can remain as such if it is acted on by external forces, because such forces affect different parts of the system differently and hence cause internal differentiation in it. Every force thus tends to bring about increasing variety. The cosmos develops from an indefinite and incoherent homogeneity to a definite and coherent inhomogeneity, representing the emergence of better and better things. Evolution, said Spencer, can only end in the establishment of the greatest perfection and most complete happiness.

Spencer's *First Principles* followed, after an interval of three years, the publication of Darwin's *Origin of the Species* (1859). Both placed emphasis on progressive evolution, with complexity and differentiation generally associated with goodness and value. However, parallel developments in physics came to the fore at about the same time. Carnot developed the basic principles of what came later to be known as the second law of thermodynamics (1824), and William Thompson stated them more forcefully in his treatise "On the Universal Tendency in Nature to the Dissipation of Mechanical Energy" (1852). On the continent, Helmholtz published his essay on the preservation of force (*Über die Erhaltung der Kraft*, 1847), and in 1865 Clausius introduced the concept of entropy. A year later Boltzmann offered a new formulation of the second law, in which it is linked with probability theory and statistical mechanics. The status of the law appeared unquestionable. And its thrust was that instead of building up, the universe as a whole is inevitably running down. Every process dissipates energy and renders it unavailable for performing work.* The great arrow of evolution points, therefore, not toward increasingly differentiated and complex things, but toward progressively disorganized, simple, and random aggregates.

The effect of the advent of thermodynamical laws on thinking about evolution in the universe was profound. The optimistic sentence concerning evolution leading to perfection and happiness, included in the first edition of Spencer's *First Principles*, is lacking in the sixth.

Despite the arguments of the physicists, it remained evident that, at least on the surface of the earth, many things continue to build up instead of running down. More recent work in astrophysics showed that even in the wider cosmos, matter is

* The reasoning behind the experimental evidence that led to the various formulations of the second law is complex and has varied throughout the nineteenth century. In its most general form it may be summed up in the argument that perpetuum-mobile machines fail necessarily, i.e., no cyclic heat engine can extract internal energy (the force capable of changing an adiabatically enclosed system from one equilibrium state to another) from a system and use it without loss in performing mechanical work. (Alternatively, without compensating changes heat cannot flow from a colder to a hotter body; according to Joule's calculations a unit of heat is equivalent to a corresponding unit of mechanical work [e.g., 778 foot-pounds $= 1$ B.T.U.].) For any change in a system from one equilibrium state to another, the heat absorbed by it $(dQ)$ may be written $dQ \leqslant TdS$, where the equality holds only for a reversible process (T stands for absolute temperature and S for entropy). Thus for a natural adiabatic process, where $dQ = O$, dS becomes positive: entropy increases. In any thermodynamic (adiabatically closed) system dS can either remain constant or increase; it can never decrease. Since maximum entropy (in thermodynamical equilibrium) is the state of highest probability in Boltzmann's statistical mechanics, and it is a state of maximum randomness or disorganization, the broader philosophic consequences of the above simple equation are considerable.

constantly building up in the course of the chemical evolution of stars and in interstellar processes associated with quasars, supernovae, and the gravitational contraction of interstellar dust. Science had to wait for the development of the thermodynamics of irreversible processes in the twentieth century, and its applications in astrophysics, biophysics, and biochemistry, to perceive that there is no contradiction between the laws of thermodynamics and the observed direction of evolution in some regions and aspects of the universe. Evolution, it turned out, exploits energy-flows which possess inherent stability in certain highly specific configurations. It takes place in open systems with inputs and outputs, whereas the laws of thermodynamics apply to closed systems. Hence the universe, as a theoretically closed system, may tend on the whole toward entropy and equilibrium; enclaves can nevertheless form within it, given large enough flows and suitable energetic conditions, which locally and temporally reverse this trend. There is no conflict with the second law—but there is no explanation by it either. We have to add further laws of the natural universe before the second law can be used to predict the evolution of complexity.

By and large, we can understand the nature of such laws at present, even if we do not have quantitative formulations beyond the first few stages of their operation. The understanding comes from the concept of "dissipative structures" advanced by scientists working in irreversible thermodynamics (Prigogine, Katchalsky, Onsager, De Groot, et al.), and from the conclusions drawn by Jacob Bronowski.[1] Dissipative structures are systems which dissipate energy in the course of their self-maintenance and self-organization. Complex entities cannot arise in nature unless there is a flow mixing the existing elements in random configurations. If all configurations had equal intrinsic stability the probability of their being maintained would be equal and described by the second law in its Boltzmannian formulation. Eventually all configurations would break down and the average pattern would bunch around the thermodynamic equilibrium state. But it appears that the flows have intrinsic stability in specific configurations. For example, protons and neutrons build enduring, stable nuclei. They can be balanced by shells of electrons, giving stable atoms. A helium atom is stable, but the configuration resulting from the thermal collision of two helium atoms is not. The structure would disintegrate in about a millionth of a microsecond. But, if during that time a third helium atom enters the configuration, a stable structure results: the nucleus of carbon. This serves as a simple physical model for the understanding of how increasingly complex structures can come about through the chance rearrangements of components in a flow. Atoms make molecules and crystals, macromolecules are composed of simpler molecules and of crystalline elements, and the simplest forms of life are composed of relatively stable configurations of the already established macromolecular aggregates. For example, the base molecules of living things, i.e., thymine, adenine, cytosine, and guanine, are stable configurations of macromolecules built into likewise stable configurations of nucleic acids. Nucleic acids in recurrent patterns code the build-up of organic phenotypes. Cells are stable configurations as self-contained units, capable of self-maintenance (metabolism) and continuity (reproduction). But they in turn can be structured into complex multicellular organisms having the basic properties of life on their own level of organization. We can carry the process still further, and find that self-contained populations find coordinations of relatively stable sorts in interspecific structures (known as ecosystems) and that local structures of this kind are coordinated in more encompassing ones, leading to the concept of the ecosphere as a complex interdetermined system. Man is a system on one level of this emergent hierarchy, and his environment is composed of its other levels.

Two general conditions make for the build-up of systems,

notwithstanding the validity of the second law. The first is a flow of energy entering the evolving region as a whole (in our case, from the sun); the second, the natural selection which hits upon, through chance variations, intrinsically stable configurations of energy-flows and matches one such configuration against and with another. If we allow that there are actual or potential configurations of energy-flows in the universe which are intrinsically stable, we get a *bona fide* explanation of the build-up of complexity. The second law becomes a law of evolution if we add to it the repertory of configurations which, when hit upon, manifest a degree of stability. Such configurations bias the statistics upon which the second law is based: random fluctuations induced by energy winds will not have thermodynamical equilibrium as their average, but the stable configuration. Hence we get a new average which serves as the starting point of fluctuations that involve the chance that further configurations of stability are hit upon, made up of the existing stable configurations as their components. Thus atoms can build into molecules, and molecules into the building blocks of life. Living species can build into ecosystems and ecosystems into the system of the ecosphere.

The new general systems concept of evolution allows that the second law of thermodynamics is an adequate description of the real universe only if it is integrated with the concept of "hidden" or "potential" strata of stability upon which the flow can hit. Every system we encounter in nature is the actualization of some such stratum of stability. This includes man, the organs and cells in his body, the molecules in the cells, and the atoms in the molecules. It includes any and all naturally constituted multiorganic systems, such as ecologies. In this class come some varieties of social systems and the world system. The result of evolution on earth is a multilevel hierarchy which encompasses atoms on the one end and large-scale multiorganic systems on the other. The higher systems are composed of integrated sets of lower-level systems. Systemic interactions among systems yield higher systemic units; other types of interactions produce differentiation and lead to speciation. The processes of evolution proceed from a state of partly ordered chaos—energy fluxes interacting with some relatively stable configurations of flows. Given a matrix with such types of order, evolution will tend toward higher levels of organization in structures of greater complexity. Disturbances affecting existing systems lead to the merging of some dynamic properties, the differentiation of others, and result in the selective evolution of systems progressively fitted to their environment. Systems evolve by adding weaker bonded components to the already strongly bonded ones, as atoms are electronically bonded in molecules, molecules in complex polymers and macromolecular structures, these in turn in cellular units, cells in tissues and multicellular systems, and multicellular individuals in ecological and social systems.*

## Systemic Invariance

The dissipative structures which emerge in the process of evolution in the ecosphere of the earth exhibit basic invariances of structure and function, notwithstanding the fact that they are diverse in appearance and seem to differ greatly in behavior. The invariances result from the shared situation and common origin of the systems: they are dynamic open systems that maintain themselves in an energy flow by dissipating organized energies and using the energies thus freed to counteract statistical tendencies toward energy degradation in the physical universe. Whether a system is relatively simple, composed directly of atoms or molecules; or highly complex,

* See the schematic representation of the organizational hierarchy in Figure 1, Chapter 2.

constituted of multiple strands of ordered relationships among already complex multicellular organisms, it must respect the universe's general conditions of self-sustenance. The manner in which particular systems do so is very different, and at first sight no comparison seems possible between them. Yet when we reconstitute the structural characteristics and functional dynamics of the various manifest properties, we find that they exhibit the invariances associated with systemic existence. Four such basic system invariances are discussed here; they are basic factors in our understanding of the unity which underlies phenomenal diversity, and which now promises fresh insights also for our understanding of that most diverse and complex system, the global system, and its own patterns of world order.

1. *Order and irreducibility*. "Order" in a system refers to the invariance that underlies its transformations of state, and by means of which the system's structure can be identified. A stable atom manifests order in the relation of its electrons to its nucleus, and a social system manifests it in the relations of its members. These relations, in atoms as well as societies, can undergo transformations: a hydrogen atom can undergo fusion and become part of a helium atom minus a radiated surplus of energy; an independent state can become federated with or assimilated into larger polities, with or without eliciting a stream of emigrants. Inasmuch as we can speak of a system as a "something" that endures long enough to identify it, and recurs often enough to have a name, we are speaking of some elements of order that are characteristic of it. We can speak of this world order or that, but inasmuch as we can identify different varieties of world order, we speak of a (real or imagined) system that has invariant structural features. The opposite of order is chaos, and the total lack of determination informing a set of elements. Absolute chaos, as well as absolute order, are abstractions; real-world systems manifest some finite degree of order, ranged between a state of mini-

mum determination and maximum (but not complete) chaos (typified by the motion of molecules in a gas), and a state of maximum (but not complete) determination and minimum chaos (for example, the behavior of a well-built machine). Systems are not necessarily "better," the more ordered they are; there is no correlation between positive value judgments and degrees of order. The concept of order is significant for our purposes as a way of identifying systems by reference to their invariant structural features, i.e., by the order of their parts. A system that has small degrees of determination will tend to undergo a rapid sequence of possibly complex transformations and poses more difficulties for the investigator than one that is highly determinate and produces few, or simple and thus highly predictable, transformations. Yet a system composed of many relatively indetermined systems does not become that much less determined itself: degrees of indeterminacy are not simply additive. In fact, any whole system we examine in the natural world is likely to be significantly more determinate as a whole than the sum of the determinacy of its parts. In other words, whole systems are more ordered than the sum of the relative disorders of their parts.* Indeed, unless this was the case, evolution would result in increasing chaos. As system interacts with system and forms a suprasystem, the individual degrees of freedom of the parts would make the whole system chaotic. However, in the real world even highly indeterminate systems can jointly compose systems with ordered characteristics. For example, in the organic body there is a constant chemical flux of complex reactions which nevertheless yields a total organism that obeys the laws

* This proposition is expressed by the formula

$$V_s << (v_a + v_b + v_c + \ldots v_n)$$

where S denotes the whole system, a, b, c, . . . n, the parts, and v stands for their degrees of variance from some given state that gives a measure of the system's order. (See Paul A. Weiss, "The Living System: Determinism Stratified," *Beyond Reductionism*, A. Koestler and J. R. Smythies, eds., London: Macmillan, 1969.)

of physiology. And in a complex sociocultural system individuals have a great deal of personal autonomy, yet the complex patterns of their interactions produce a total structure that can be grasped by the principles of the social sciences.

This takes us to the concept of irreducibility. The concept refers to certain properties of a whole system which are specific on that level, and are not the simple additions of the properties of its parts. The order of a whole system is one such property and there are others, as we shall see. However, claiming that certain properties of whole systems are not equal to the sum of the properties of their parts is not to reaffirm a mystical belief in the old adage, "The whole is more than the sum of its parts." In fact, wholes can be mathematically shown to be other than the simple sum of the properties and functions of their parts.*

Let us consider merely the following basic notions. Complexes of parts can be calculated in three distinct ways:[2]

---

\* A nonsummative complex of interdetermined elements may be represented thus:

$$\left.\begin{array}{l} \dfrac{dQ_1}{dt} = f_1 \ (Q_1, \ Q_2, \ \ldots \ Q_n) \\[2mm] \dfrac{dQ_2}{dt} = f_2 \ (Q_1, \ Q_2, \ \ldots \ Q_n) \\[2mm] \dfrac{dQ_n}{dt} = f_n \ (Q_1, \ Q_2, \ \ldots \ Q_n) \end{array}\right\}$$

In this system of simultaneous differential equations, change of any measure $Q_i$ is a function of all $Q$'s and conversely. An equation governing a change in any one part is different in form from the equation governing change in the whole. Thus the pattern of change in the whole complex is different from (is not reducible to) the patterns of change in any of its parts. However, by developing the complex into Taylor series, and assuming that the coefficients of the variables $Q_i$ become zero, it becomes summative: change in each element is unaffected by its relations to change in other elements, and the sum of the changes precisely equals the change in the whole. (Such transformation of a nonsummative into a summative complex is not possible in real-world systems without "killing" the system, i.e., destroying the dynamics which maintains it.) (See L. von Bertalanffy, *General System Theory*, New York: George Braziller, 1968, Chapter 3.)

(i) by counting the *number* of parts,
(ii) by taking into account the *species* to which the parts belong, and
(iii) by considering the *relations* between the parts

In cases (i) and (ii) the complex may be understood as the sum of the parts considered in isolation. In these cases the complex has *cumulative* characteristics: it is sufficient to sum the properties of the parts to obtain the properties of the whole. Such wholes are better known as "heaps" or "aggregates," since the fact that the parts are joined in them makes no difference to their functions—i.e., the interrelations of the parts do not qualify their joint behavior. A heap of bricks is an example of this. But consider anything from an atom to an organism or a society: the particular relations of the parts bring forth properties which are not present in (or are meaningless in reference to) the parts. Examples range from the Pauli exclusion principle in atoms (which does not say anything about individual electrons), through homeostatic self-regulation in organisms (which is meaningless in reference to individual cells or organs), all the way to distributive justice in society (likewise meaningless in regard to individual members). Each of these complexes is not a mere heap, but a whole which is *other* than the sum of its parts.

The mathematics of nonsummative complexes apply to systems of the widest variety, including physical, biological, social, and psychological systems. These systems form ordered wholes in which the law-bound regularities exhibited by interdependent elements determine the functional behavior of the totality. The fallacy of reducing a whole atom to the sum of the properties of its parts is well known to atomic physicists; the analogous fallacy of reducing the whole organism to biochemical reactions and physical properties manifested by particular components is also becoming recognized, and so is the fallacy of reducing the properties of human multiperson systems to the psychological and physiological properties of the participating members.

The irreducibility of the properties of social systems formed by human beings has been stressed by the functionalists and is acknowledged by most social scientists, with the possible exception of a few radical phenomenologists and empiricists. The holistic nature of social phenomena is evident in the study of group behavior and runs through the gamut of social entities up to and including the international level. The reductionist-mechanistic concept is inapplicable to social systems also because mechanistic systems behave in an exactly identical fashion whenever their members are disassembled and put together again irrespective of the sequence in which the disassembling and reassembling took place. But it is not the case that the members of social systems are never significantly modified by each other, or their own past, and remain interchangeable in terms of their precise function. Moreover the characteristic properties of social systems are not characteristics of the individual humans who participate in them, but arise out of their strands of interaction. Thus it is nonsense to speak of "government," "justice," "economic structure," "legal system," "political order," and the like in terms of individuals, except perhaps in a loose, metaphorical sense. Yet individuals collectively form systems to which such concepts clearly apply. The characteristics of structure and function, which render such concepts applicable to social systems and not to their individual members, constitute the irreducible properties of social systems. They are as irreducible as the corresponding properties of organisms (e.g., homeostasis, adaptation, purposive behavior, etc.) and even of atoms (such as chemical valence).

2. *Self-stabilization.* Real-world systems are exposed to environmental disturbances, yet they depend on their environments to obtain the energies needed for the coherence of their structure. Consequently viable systems exhibit a reper-

tory of self-stabilizing functions, by means of which they counteract nonlethal disturbances produced by their milieu. Self-stabilization involves a temporary (forced) departure by the system from its characteristic set of internal relations, coupled with a pronounced tendency to return to the characteristic relations when the disturbance is over. The characteristic states of the systems are its "steady-states"—they are not static states, but ones which represent a level of equilibrium between the internal constraints among the system's components and the forces acting on it from its environment. Katchalsky and Curran have shown that systems characterized by fixed internal constraints and exposed to unrestrained forces in their environment tend to produce countervailing forces that bring them back to the stable states, since the flow caused by the perturbation has the same sign as the perturbation itself.[3] Hence the effect of the flow is to reduce the perturbation, and permit the system to return to its steady-state. If the perturbations vanish, the system is again characterized by the parameters of its fixed constraints. If both the fixed and the unrestrained forces vanish, the system reaches a state of thermodynamic equilibrium—it becomes a heap, rather than a dynamically ordered whole.

In the steady-state the systems are the most economical from the energetic viewpoint since they lose the minimum amount of free energy. (A still more economical state is the state of thermodynamic equilibrium; in that state, however, the systems are no longer ordered wholes.) Minimum entropy production characterizes the complex systems we term "living," which slow down the process of thermodynamic decay during their lifetime and remain in a sequence of time-dependent steady-states characterized by the typical constraints making up the species-specific organization of the individual. Such systems possess regulating mechanisms that preserve the steady-state and bring the organism back to its unperturbed condition in a way which resembles the action of a restoring force coming into play in any fluctuation from a stationary state in a physical system. Inasmuch as both physical and biological systems maintain themselves in steady-states characterized by the parameters of their internal forces, life as a cybernetic process is analogous to any physical system describable, by our definition, as endowed with the dynamics of self-stabilization.

Self-stabilization occurs by means of stereotyped function performance in relatively mechanistic systems, and through synergistic, simultaneous mutual regulation of the parts in most other varieties of systems. The paradigm of stereotyped self-stabilization is the negative-feedback mechanism consisting of sensor, effector, correlator, and regulator components with a unidirectional circular flow among them.* The exact nature of the causal dynamics responsible for syngeristic simultaneous regulations of parts in a nonmechanistic system is not fully known, but recent investigations suggest that continuous fields rather than atomistic causal chains may be involved, and that the phenomenon known as inductive resonance may have a role to play.†

* The standard design of a negative-feedback mechanism in terms of its basic information flow is the following:

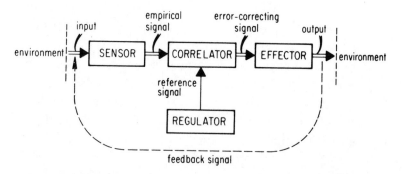

FIGURE IX

The above flow diagram is given in a somewhat more sophisticated form in Figure VI, Chapter 5, above.

† Weiss points out that whenever one group of components in a system deviates from its standard course, the rest automatically change course so as to

In complex systems negative feedback self-regulation can involve multiple loops and constitute sensitive adaptive mechanisms. The principles underlying self-regulation through the feedback of information on the system's behavior can be gleaned from recent experiences with so-called learning machines or nets. In the simplest of such machines no element is so placed that its output forms part of the input of another adjustable element (for example, in the "simple Perceptron"[4]). The principle according to which adjustments are made is thus very simple, because every adjustable element contributes to the final output in a direct way—there is no need to determine in advance the current sensitivity of the output to changes in that element. However, in more complex artificial systems adaptive changes are not restricted to a single functional layer. The system can incorporate special information pathways carrying signals back from the point at which the final output leaves the net.[5] These signals can provide, at every point in the net, a continuous measure of the sensitivity of the output to activity at that point. This measure

---

counteract the distortion of the pattern of the whole. But how do the components know what happens elsewhere in the system, and how to act appropriately? Since the number of possible departures from an ideal standard course is infinite, the number of corrective responses potentially called for from each component is likewise infinite. The problem is further compounded by the number of subunits involved in the collective response. Faced without hedging, says Weiss, this problem patently defies solution in terms of the "cooperation" of atomistic, free and independent components. Instead, we must switch to the concept of *field continua*. ("The Basic Concept of Hierarchic Systems," in: *Hierarchically Organized Systems in Theory and Practice*, Paul A. Weiss, *et al*, New York: Hafner, 1971).

Although the question of stabilization around dynamically stable integral configurations in complex systems is still not clearly answered, one possible solution may lie in an extension of the phenomenon of inductive resonance. Inductive resonance was discovered by Huygens in the seventeenth century when he observed that two clocks which were slightly out of phase when fixed to a solid wall became synchronized when attached to a thin wooden board. The finding was ignored until Van der Pol explained it in 1922 as inductive coupling due to heteroperiodic resonance. The principal effect is the synchronization of slightly out-of-step oscillators under mutual influence. It is found to occur in the energy transfer in photosynthesis between chlorophyll *a* and *b*, in the synchronization of the flashes of fireflies, in the action of electronic pace-makers on the heart, in the adjustment of alpharhythms to

can be used, along with the measure of the deviation of the final output from a normed value, to determine adjustments made at that point.*

In most kinds of natural systems, relatively stereotyped negative feedback mechanisms and relatively spontaneous and holistic simultaneous self-regulations are intertwined, although one mode of operation may be vastly more important

---

stroboscopic flashes perceived through the eye; some investigators now suggest that it may be basic to the self-regulation of complex biochemical systems (cf., Brian C. Goodwin, "A Statistical Mechanics of Temporal Organization in Cells," *Towards a Theoretical Biology*, C. H. Waddington, ed. Chicago: Aldine, 1969, 141–163; A. S. Iberall, S. Cardon, A. Schindler, F. Yates and D. Marsh, "Progress Toward the Application of Systems Science Concepts to Biology," Arlington, Va.: Army Research Office, September 1972, 65–68).

* To see how such information feedback could operate, and what sort of system is needed to implement it, consider an element of the net whose inputs are signals $x(t)$ and $y(t)$, varying with time, and the output $z(t)$ is the result of multiplying these together. There is a feedback signal $s(t)$ associated with the pathway conveying the signal $z(t)$. If this is the final output of the net, then $s(t) = 1$ at all times. An appropriate feedback signal to be associated with the upper input pathway is $s(t) \cdot y(t)$, since the degree to which the output is sensitive to activity in this channel is proportional to $y(t)$. A feedback signal $s(t) \cdot x(t)$ is associated similarly with the lower input channel. The system component which performs the multiplication of the forward-going signals $x(t)$ and $y(t)$ incorporates the means of performing appropriate operations on the feedback signals. If all elements operate in this dual way, an information-feedback signal is made available throughout the system. (Data supplied by A. M. Andrew.)

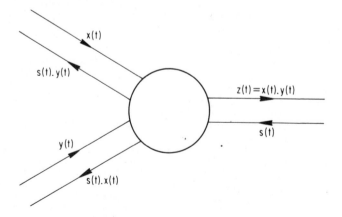

FIGURE X

than the other. For example, in the regulation of cellular activity in simpler species of organisms (lacking an evolved nervous system) resonance induced by the biochemical locking or entrainment of oscillators may be the principal mechanism of self-regulation, whereas in formally organized human societies the institutionally performed negative-feedback control of all relevant inputs and outputs (manufacture and dumping of products, demands and decisions, energy sources and sinks, etc.) is the decisive agency of control and stability.

Systems stabilize themselves around dynamic steady-states by means of a variety of mechanisms and processes, the possibilities for which are determined by the nature of their components and the level of their integration within the systemic whole. But regardless of what process or mechanism is used to perform the stabilizing functions, we may note that self-stabilization is effectively accomplished by systems on all principal levels of organization. On the supraorganic level it is manifested by systems that may be inter- or intra-specific. Most ecosystems are interspecific, whereas social systems are intraspecific. Intraspecific social systems occur among various species, but the complex forms obtain among insects and vertebrates. The most complex and sophisticated social systems are produced by our species; these are distinguished by the *sui generis* elements of language and culture. Regardless of the differences, however, all such systems maintain themselves over time and, inasmuch as their structural characteristics do not change despite variations in their environment, they manifest the dynamics of steady-state self-stabilization in one form or another.

Functionalist sociologists use the concept of "equilibrium" to define the stabilized states in human sociocultural systems. (By this they do not mean *thermodynamical* equilibrium, however.) They view social organizations as open systems with self-regulating mechanisms maintaining the equilibrium states of the system within definite limits. In order to survive, the system has needs fulfilled by its parts or components. These define their "function." According to functionalists, every part of a social system should be interpreted and analyzed from the perspective of the contribution it makes to the survival and adaptation of the whole system.

Because of its emphasis on self-stabilization, functionalism has been criticized for leading to a conservative bias: if all existing institutions contribute toward the survival needs of a social system, they are all valuable on that account. But regardless of the warrant for such criticism (which has been partially answered by general systems theorists who have also described social systems processes of self-*organization*), it is clear that the phenomenon of self-stabilization is manifested in social, not only biological, systems, and that in the social realm it is manifested through mechanisms that conserve established patterns: rituals, mores, law enforcement, political conservatism, traditionalism, and so on.

3. *Self-organization.* A number of different cybernetic and systems models have now been produced to account for the phenomenon of self-organization.[6] It is fair to say, however, that except in the case of relatively simple systems (mainly artificial ones), the principles of self-organization are not understood in detail. How, for example, the very information which codes a genotype is generated in the course of phylogenetic evolution is still not satisfactorily explained. Nevertheless, some general principles did come to light. First, it now appears that self-organization necessarily involves an open system (or a system coupled with another system) and can never take place in an isolated system. Second, self-organization presupposes some inputs from the system's environment which stress or stimulate the system in some way, i.e., which have the overall effect of perturbations. If, however, a system has experienced a long and complex series of perturbations in its evolutionary history, it may develop random or residual

innovative activity (such as mutations in a genotype or spontaneous innovations in a culture) which diversify populations of systems and keep them adapted to a wide range of possible environmental perturbations. Third, it is now understood that self-organization occurs in systems that have multiple equilibria or, what is the same thing in different words, several strata of potential stability. In view of these findings, self-organization can be explained on the general evolutionary principle of fluctuations induced either by energy-flows in the milieu acting on systems or by spontaneous activity by the systems themselves, inducing chance variations of states, some of which hit upon levels of stability. This principle makes self-organization a nonrandom yet nonteleological process, governed by the interplay of chance fluctuations of state and determinate levels of potential stability. It respects the characteristic principles of self-organization: openness in the systems, perturbing environmental inputs or self-induced variations, and multiple levels of potential stability.

The fact that self-organization occurs in a system does not conflict with the laws of thermodynamics, as previously argued. It can even be expressed in the language of irreversible thermodynamics.* Consequently there is nothing mysterious or supernatural about the fact of systemic self-organization, even if its detailed workings in complex real-world systems are not yet adequately understood. It is the system property which permits populations of systems to evolve, and to create the rich diversity of phenomena in the world. Without self-organizing systems the universe would still not have progressed beyond its chemical elements—and even the build-up

---

* The Prigogine equation states that entropy change in a system is governed by the relative values of the terms in the equation, $dS = dS_e + dS_i$, where $dS_i$ denotes entropy change through the input and $dS_e$ entropy produced through irreversible processes within the system. Whereas $dS_e$ is always positive, $dS_i$ may be positive as well as negative. If it is negative, the dissipation function of a system ($\Psi = ds/dt$) is negative, i.e., $\Psi < 0$. In that case, the system decreases its net entropy or, what is the same thing, gathers information ($\Psi < 0$) = (d info/dt > 0).

of the elements is an instance of progressive self-organization, on the most basic physical level.[7]

The particular mechanism through which self-organizing expresses itself varies with the level of complexity and evolutionary history of the systems. In biological systems the principal mechanism of self-organization is mutation in the genotype coupled with environmental selection acting on the phenotype. In sociocultural systems self-organization occurs by means of innovative changes induced by members of a society, either to better cope with internal or external perturbations, or to extend their control capacity over the rest of the social system or its social and natural environment. The development of new technologies, both hardware and software, calls for a modified social structure that is more adapted than previous structures for handling the new system-environment relations. Threats to the safety or identity of a social system likewise trigger a defensive reorganization of structures and functions. Sociocultural evolution occurs because of the capacity of viable social systems to respond to external challenges and to internal innovations through self-organization, much as biological evolution is rendered possible by the ability of the genotype to undergo adaptively advantageous mutations.

Independently of the local mechanisms responsible for the processes, we can say that, in general, self-organization conduces systems toward more negentropic states, and self-stabilization maintains them in their preexisting level and state of organization. If the systems have some residual innovative capacity, or if perturbations are continuously operating on them in their environment, systems not only survive, but evolve. The evolution of systems can then be conceptualized as a sequence of parallel, or irregularly alternating, stabilization around the parameters of their existing fixed forces (defining the steady-states), and the reorganization of the fixed forces for increasing adaptation to changes in the systems' internal or external environment.

4. *Hierarchization*. Whenever a set of self-stabilizing and self-organizing systems share a common environment, their patterns of evolution crystallize some strands of mutual adaptations. Some varieties of system may evolve specialized functions within cooperative networks of relations. The network formed by the mutually adapted functions may likewise represent the realization of a potential level of stability, though on a superordinate level, and may be conceptualized as a system in its own right. Such a system can interact with other systems on its own superordinate level, and form still higher-level suprasystems through the evolutionary crystallization of their own mutual adaptations. Systems on every level may exhibit the general properties of order, irreducibility, homeostatic self-stabilization, and evolutionary self-organization. The apex of any such hierarchy is itself a system, of which all other systems are subsystems.

That evolutionary development proceeds in a hierarchical fashion can be clearly understood by reference to Simon's calculations.[8] These show that a system composed of independently stable subsystems can withstand perturbations to a significantly higher degree than systems built directly from their components. Hence hierarchical systems are more stable in a changing milieu, and there is an overwhelming probability that surviving real-world systems possess a hierarchical structure. Indeed, such structure is exhibited by existing systems in the biological as well as the social realm. Whatever living system we analyze, we find hierarchical order in descending steps from the whole system down to the most basic subsystem. For instance, complex whole organisms are composed of major parts, such as limbs, and principal organ systems, such as the respiratory system. Each of these systems is further composed of relatively stable subsystems. Limbs are not built directly from their contingent of cells, but cells in groups establish unit sublimb structures such as a skeletal element or a muscle. These in turn constitute limb parts such as toes, and all such parts in concert yield the unit limb. One can further go beyond the cells down to its parts: the organelle, the macromolecular system, the macromolecule, the constituent chemical molecules, and the atoms themselves. Although the higher units cannot exist outside the context of the integrated whole organism, the lower units can. Moreover the morphogenesis of the organism follows the paths of unit-construction and assembly, capitalizing on the coherence and integration of the already constituted subunits.

We can also analyze a social system and find that its many subsystems form relatively stable assemblies. Political systems, for example, are composed of principal institutional structures with established, relatively stable functions. The institutions themselves are segmented into bureaus and departments, each with distinct responsibilities and resources. Although here, too, the higher substructures may depend on the whole system for viability, lower-level bureaucratic units are independently stable: they are maintained regardless of changes at the top. Hierarchical organization assures continuity and therewith stability in a political system. Similar observations hold, *mutatis mutandis*, for the economic, cultural, military, industrial, agricultural, and other domains of sociocultural systems.

That development generally proceeds in a hierarchical fashion explains many otherwise puzzling phenomena. It tells us that in complex systems different descriptions will apply to different levels of structure and function. For example, we get different descriptions when we concentrate on the organ, the cell, the organelle, the macromolecule, and the atom in an organism. We also get different descriptions when we examine an entire political system, its particular institutional components, and its specialized bureaus and departments. The hierarchical nature of development tells us that there will be greater diversity of structure and function at the higher levels than at the lower ones. The higher levels are made up of many lower-level systems plus all their interrelations. New functions and structures can thus emerge at each higher level, and these are specific transformations of basic invariances found on all levels. For example, homeostasis as well as ethical conservatism are self-stabilizing functions in systems, but are expressed in qualitatively different forms. Revolutionary movements and mutations are both elements in processes of self-organization, exposed to the test of natural selection, but they too assume very different manifest forms. The properties emerging at successive levels in hierarchical systems are irreducible transformations of the systems invariances that hold true on all levels.

Last but not least, we understand that greater diversity at higher levels goes hand in hand with smaller populations at these levels. There are fewer cells than molecules, fewer organisms than cells, and fewer societies than organisms. Ultimately there is but one global ecosystem which, together with its human components, forms the world system which is the principal object of this inquiry.

# NOTES

---

## Chapter 1

1. Cf. the study by the Center for the Study of Social Policy of the Stanford Research Institute, directed by O. W. Markley, "Changing Images of Man." Discussion Draft, 1973 (in mimeographed form). Chapter 1.

2. Albert Einstein, *The World As I See It*. New York: Covici–Friede, 1934. 138.

3. Werner Heisenberg, *Philosophic Problems of Nuclear Science*. London: Faber and Faber, 1952. 94.

4. Cf. Ervin Laszlo and Henry Margenau, "The Emergence of Integrative Concepts in Contemporary Science," *Philosophy of Science*, Spring 1972.

5. Cf. Thomas S. Kuhn, *The Structure of Scientific Revolutions*. Chicago: University of Chicago Press, 1970. Chapter IV.

6. James B. Conant, *Modern Science and Modern Man*. New York: Doubleday–Anchor, 1952. 105.

7. Ludwig von Bertalanffy, *General System Theory*. New York: George Braziller, 1968. 38.

8. Prospectus of the Society for General Systems Research, Washington, D.C.

9. Cf. the *General Systems Yearbooks*, annually since 1956; the issues of *Behavioral Science*, a journal of the Society for General Systems Research since 1973; *Trends in General Systems Theory*, G. Klir, ed. New York: Wiley, 1972; and *The Relevance of General Systems Theory*, E. Laszlo, ed. New York: George Braziller, 1973.

# Chapter 2

1. James B. Conant, *Modern Science and Modern Man*, op. cit.

2. Harold Sprout and Margaret Sprout, *Toward a Politics of the Planet Earth*. New York: Von Nostrand Reinhold, 1971; Jay W. Forrester, *World Dynamics*. Cambridge, Mass.: Wright–Allen, 1971; D. H. Meadows, D. L. Meadows, J. Randers and W. W. Behrens III, *The Limits to Growth*. New York: Universe Books, 1972.

3. C. Wright Mills, *The Sociological Imagination*. New York: Oxford University Press, 1959. 135, 136.

4. Richard A. Falk, *This Endangered Planet*. New York: Random House, 1971. 37ff.

5. See for example *Linkage Politics*, James Rosenau, ed. New York: The Free Press, 1969; and the *World Order Models Project Manuscripts*, sponsored by the Institute for World Order, New York, with research teams operating in many parts of the world.

6. J. David Singer, "The Level of Analysis Problem in International Relations," *The International System*, Klaus Knorr and Sidney Verba, eds. Princeton: Princeton University Press, 1961. 77–92.

7. Robert K. Merton, *Social Theory and Social Structure*. Glencoe, Ill.: Free Press of Glencoe, 1957. 49.

8. Richard A. Falk, "Reforming World Order: Zones of Consciousness and Domains of Action," *The World System: Models, Norms, Applications*, E. Laszlo, ed. New York: George Braziller, 1973.

9. For details see Alastair M. Taylor, "The Political Implications of the Forrester World System Model," *The World System: Models, Norms, Applications*, op. cit.

10. Cf. Jacob Bronowski, "New Concepts in the Evolution of Complexity," *Zygon*, Vol. 5 (1), March 1970. 18–35.

11. Klaus Krippendorf, "Communication and the Genesis of Structure," *General System Yearbook*, XVI (1971). 171.

12. Ervin Laszlo, *Introduction to Systems Philosophy*. New York: Harper Torchbooks, 1973. 38 ff.

13. Walter Buckley, *Sociology and Modern Systems Theory*. Englewood Cliffs: Prentice–Hall, 1967. 58–66.

14. *Ibid.* 63.

15. Alastair M. Taylor, "Some Political Implications of the Forrester World System Model," *The World System: Models, Norms, Applications*, op. cit.

16. *Ibid.*

17. See Alastair M. Taylor, *Societies in History: A Systems Approach*. New York: George Braziller (forthcoming).

18. Henry A. Kissinger, "Domestic Structure and Foreign Policy," *Con-*

*ditions of World Order*, Stanley Hoffman, ed. Boston: Houghton Mifflin, 1968. 190.

19. Abraham A. Maslow, *Motivation and Personality*. New York: Harper, 1954.

20. Cf. Richard A. Falk, *This Endangered Planet*, op. cit. 229f.

21. Kenneth E. Boulding, "The Shadow of the Stationary State," *Daedalus*, Fall 1973. 92.


## Chapter 3


1. Martin Abend on the Ten O'Clock News, WNEW–TV. May 28, 1973.

2. Cf. Albert D. Biderman, "The Image of 'Brainwashing'," *Public Opinion Quarterly*, Vol. 26 (1962); E. Cumming and J. Cumming, *Closed Ranks: An Experiment in Mental Health Education*. Cambridge, Mass.: Harvard University Press, 1957.

3. Cf. Kissinger, op. cit.

4. Jørgen Randers and Donella H. Meadows, "The Carrying Capacity of Our Global Environment: A Look at the Ethical Alternatives," *Towards Global Equilibrium: Collected Papers*. Cambridge, Mass: Wright–Allen, 1973.

5. Cf. Ervin Laszlo, *System, Structure and Experience*. New York and London: Gordon and Breach, 1969. Chapter 3.


## Chapter 4


1. Garrett Hardin, "The Tragedy of the Commons," *Science*, Vol. 162 (December 13, 1968). 1243–1248.

2. See, for example, W. Warren Wagar, *Building the City of Man: Outlines of a World Civilization*. New York: Grossman, 1971.


## Chapter 5


1. B. F. Skinner, *Beyond Freedom and Dignity*. New York: Knopf, 1971.

2. José Delgado, *Physical Control of the Mind: Toward a Psychocivilized Society*. New York: Harper & Row, 1969.

3. Kenneth B. Clark, "Psychotechnology and the Pathos of Power," *American Psychologist*, December 1971. 1047–1057.

4. L. Festinger, *A Theory of Cognitive Dissonance*. Evanston, Ill.: Row, Peterson, 1957.

5. Paul A. Weiss, *Hierarchically Organized Systems in Theory and Practice.* New York: Hafner, 1971. Chapter 1.

6. See the materials made available by the Resource Science Centre of the University of British Columbia, and the Greater Vancouver Regional District office. Also see "An Urban Systems Model for Greater Vancouver" by M. E. Turner, in *Proceedings* of the NATO Conference on the Cybernetic Modeling of Adaptive Organizations, 1973.

7. Cf. Amitai Etzioni, "MINERVA: An Electronic Townhall," *Policy Sciences*, Vol. 3 (4). 457–474.

## Chapter 6

1. The idea originates with Walter B. Cannon, in the last chapter of *The Wisdom of the Body.* New York: W. W. Norton, 1932.

2. Cf. K. Samuelson, "World-Wide Information Networks," *Conference on Interlibrary Communications and Information Networks.* Chicago: American Library Association, 1970.

3. Cf. Harold Sprout and Margaret Sprout, *Toward a Politics of the Planet Earth,* op. cit.

## Chapter 7

1. Cf. Karl W. Deutsch, *The Nerves of Government.* New York: The Free Press, 1966. Chapter 11.

## Appendix

1. Cf. T. Prigogine. *Etude Thermodynamique des Phenomènes Irreversibles.* Paris, 1947; A. Katchalsky and P. F. Curran, *Nonequilibrium Thermodynamics in Biophysics.* Cambridge, Mass.: Harvard University Press, 1965; A. Katchalsky, "Thermodynamics of Flow and Biological Organization," *Zygon*, Vol. 6 (2), June 1971. 99–125; Jacob Bronowski, "New Concepts in the Evolution of Complexity," *Zygon*, Vol. 5 (1), March 1970. 18–35.

2. Cf. Ludwig von Bertalanffy, *General System Theory*, op. cit. 54 f.

3. A. Katchalsky and P. F. Curran, *Nonequilibrium Thermodynamics in Biophysics*, op. cit. Chapter 16.

4. N. J. Nilsson, *Learning Machines.* New York: McGraw–Hill, 1965. Chapter 5.

5. A. M. Andrew, "Significance Feedback and Redundancy Reduction in

Self–Organizing Networks," F. Pichler and R. Trappl, eds., *Advances in Cybernetics and Systems Research*. London: Transcripta Books, 1973. Vol. 1.

6.   See, for example, *Principles of Self-Organization*, Heinz von Foerster and George W. Zopf, eds. New York: Pergamon, 1962. Also consult Norbert Wiener, *Cybernetics*. Cambridge, Mass.: MIT Press, 1961; W. Ross Ashby, *An Introduction to Cybernetics*. New York: Barnes & Noble, 1956; and *Design for a Brain*. London: Chapman and Hall, 1952.

7.   Cf. Ervin Laszlo, *Introduction to Systems Philosophy*, op. cit. 63–66.

8.   Herbert A. Simon, "The Architecture of Complexity," *Proceedings of the American Philosophical Society*, 106 (1962).

# Index

Actual-State Boards, 158, 159
Analytic method, 12
Art, 99–101

*Bertalanffy, Ludwig von,* 15
Biofeedback, 116–119
*Boltzmann, L.,* 205
*Boulding, K.,* 59
*Bronowski, J.,* 206
*Buckley, W.,* 35

*Cannon, W.,* 145
*Carnot, S.,* 204
Capitalism, 86
Central guidance system, 59–60,
    143–182
*Clark, K.,* 113
*Clausius, R.,* 205
Cognitive dissonance theory, 115
*Conant, J. B.,* 21
Conceptual synthesis, 3–15, 20
    functions of, 7, 8
Concern for future, 79–80
*Condorcet, M.,* 5
Consciousness, 31
Consensus, 67–69, 73, 85
Council of Principals, 160–161
Counterculture groups, 93–94
Cybernetics concepts, 185–187
Cybernetics I and II, 35–36, 38

*Darwin, Ch.,* 204
Decision-makers, 76

*Delgado, J.,* 113
Dissipative structures, 206–209

Ecofeedback, 111–142
    response mechanism, 129–132
*Einstein, A.,* 12
Energy-flow circuits, 149–152
Environmental load, 70–71
Equilibrium, 219
Evolution, 31–33, 203–208
    sociocultural, 33–43, 222
Executive Coordinating Board,
    164–166
Executive Grievance System, 175–
    176

*Falk, R. A.,* 23, 27, 85n., 152n.
Feasibility research, 161–165
Finite world, 48
Foreign policies, 74–78
*Forrester, J.,* 29, 80
*Frye, N.,* v

General Systems Theory, xiv, 15–
    20, 28–41, 117
    hypotheses of, 203–225
Geopolitical systems, 40
Global civilization, 7
Global homeostasis, 34, 143–200
    need for, 183–184
    strategies of, 184–185
Global information network, 132–
    134, 153–154

Global reform, vii, viii
Growth ideology, 49–50, 94

Hardin, G., 15, 86
Heaps, 213
Heisenberg, W., 12
Helmholtz, H., 204 ,205
Hierarchization, 223–225
History, 41–42
Hobbes, Th., 56, 57
Holbach, P., 5
Humanism, 47–48, 61
Human needs, 43–47, 120–121, 123
Hume, D., 5

Implementation Research Board, 161–165
Individuals, world-order role, 65–83
Inductive resonance, 216–217
Information feedback, 218n.
Information-flow circuits, 152–176
Information technology, 137–138
Intellectual elites, 105–106
International civil servants, 89–90, 96–97
International relations, 22
Invariance, systemic, 33–34, 209–225
Invisible-hand doctrine, 86
Irreducibility, 201–214

Kissinger, H., 42
Krippendorf, K., 32

Lamettrie, J. de, 5
Laszlo, E., v–ix
Lenin, V. I., 6
Level of analysis, 23–26

Levels of systems, 32, 223–225
Lévi-Strauss, C., 29
Lifestyle, 69–72
Literature, 99–101

Marx, K., 6
Maslow, A. H., 45
Material technics, 37, 55
Meadows, D., 80
Merton, R., 27
Mills, C. W., 22
MINERVA, 139–140
Morphogenesis, 35–36
Morphostasis, 35–36
Multiechelon system, 132
Multilevel decisions, 111
Multinational corporations, 91–92, 101

Nation-state, xiii, 22, 24, 41, 51–52, 87
Need hierarchy, 45–47
Negative-feedback mechanism, 216–218
Normative world, 119–129
Norms, 9, 19, 26, 125–127

Oil, 71
Optimum state, 50, 123, 194–197
Optimum-State Board, 159–160
Optimum-State Policy Review Court, 160
Optimum-State Steering Committee, 157–160
Order, 210–213

Political participation, 72–73, 112, 129–132, 134
Population, 121–123
Postindustrial society, xiii, xiv

Progressive leadership, 107–108
Psychocivilization of society, 113–114
Public information, 112, 124–142
Public media, 103–104, 106–107
Purpose, sense of, 9

Randers, J., 80
Relevance tree analysis, 26–127
Rights, individual and national, 177–178

Scenario of future developments, vii
Science, 9–15
   applied, 14
   policy, 14
   social, 21
Scientific knowledge, 8–9, 11
Scientific synthesis, 9–15
Self-organization, 34–35, 220–223
Self-stabilization, 34–35, 214–220
Simon, H., 223
Simulation, 119–129
Singer, D., 25
Skinner, B. F., 113
Societal technics, 37, 55
Society, concepts of, 28–30, 56–57
Society for General Systems Research, 16
Social contract, 29, 57
Social Darwinism, 30
Social system, 28–29
Sociocultural system, 33–41
Sovereignty, 41, 51–52
Specialization, 12–15
Spencer, H., 204, 205
Sprout, H., xv
Steady state, 49, 193–194, 215
Strata of stability, 207–209
Strategy for the future, xiv et passim

Strategy of popular involvement, 65–83
Structure, 17
System, 17–18
   artificial, 18
   natural, 18–19
Systems philosophy, xiv, xv

Taylor, A. M., 36
Thermodynamics, 204–206
   of irreversible processes, 206, 221
   second law of, 204–205
Thompson, W., 204
Townhall meeting, vii, 130–132
Tragedy of the Commons, 86

United Nations, 141
   organizations, 89–90
Utopianism, v, vi

Values, 82–83, 112–113, 115–116

Wiener, N., 186
World Ecological Authority, 173–174
World Ecological Information Agency, 173
World Ecology Court, 176
World Ecology Monitor, 155–156
World Economic Advisory Service, 168–169
World Economic System, 167–169
World Economy Monitor, 155
World Executive Services, 166–176
World Government, 56–59
World Health Organization, 171–172

World Homeostat System, 143–182
  components, 147
  design, 145–148, 187
  efficiency, 187–192
  funding, 178
  personnel, 179–180
  physical plant, 180
World Information Coordinating Board, 156–157
World Information Services, 153–154
World model, 124–125
World Monetary and Tax Policy Council, 169–170
World Monetary and Tax Policy Court, 175–176
World order, xiv, xv, 7, 19, 27, 55, 61
  general systems theory of, 28–41
  norms, 41, 61
  studies, vi
  theories of, 21–26

World Population Information Agency, 170–171
World Population Monitor, 155
World Rescue Organization, 174–175
World Revenue Service, 149–151
World Security Court, 175
World Security Forces, 166–167
World system, 22, 24–25
World system consciousness, 84–110
  achievers, 93–95
  disseminators, 88–93
  era of, 85
  raising, vii, viii, 84–110
World System for Ecological Balance, 172–174
World Treasury, 151–152

Zero Economic Growth, 49, 193
Zero Population Growth, 49–193